Invisible Journeys
Communication

Caroline Grimshaw

TEXT EDITOR IQBAL HUSSAIN
SCIENCE CONSULTANT JOHN STRINGER

in association with

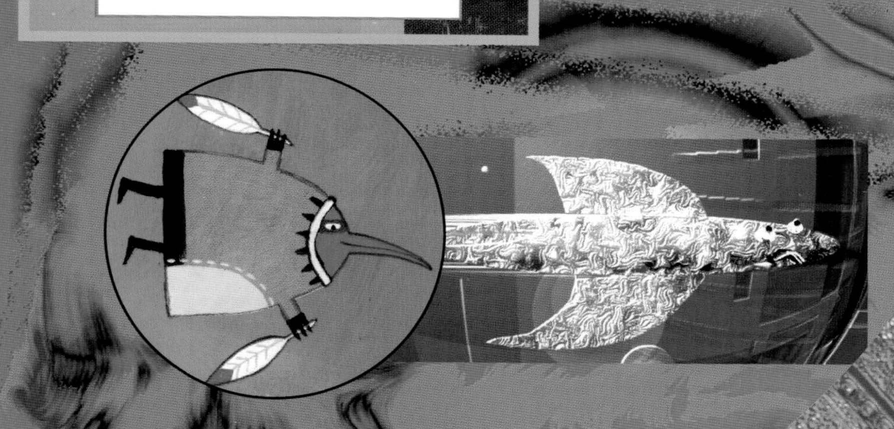

Invisible Journeys

Communication

CREATIVE AND EDITORIAL DIRECTOR
CONCEPT/FORMAT/DESIGN/TEXT
CAROLINE GRIMSHAW

TEXT EDITOR
IQBAL HUSSAIN

SCIENCE CONSULTANT
JOHN STRINGER UNIVERSITY OF WARWICK, U.K.

ILLUSTRATIONS
NICK DUFFY ✻ SPIKE GERRELL
CAROLINE GRIMSHAW

THANKS TO
PATRICIA OHLENROTH U.S. EDITOR

✻ SUN
✻ COMMUNICATION

FIRST PUBLISHED IN THE UNITED STATES AND CANADA BY
WORLD BOOK, INC.
525 W. MONROE
CHICAGO, IL 60661
IN ASSOCIATION WITH TWO-CAN PUBLISHING LTD.

FOR INFORMATION ON OTHER WORLD BOOK PRODUCTS, CALL 1-800-255-1750, EXT. 2238, OR VISIT US AT OUR WEB SITE AT HTTP://WWW.WORLDBOOK.COM

ISBN: 0-7166-3001-X (PBK.) 0-7166-3000-1 (HBK.)

LC: 97-61496

PRINTED IN HONG KONG.
1 2 3 4 5 6 7 8 9 10 01 00 99 98 97

I am your Route Scout. I will take you on your journey. Watch for my two companions.

Welcome TO Invisible Journeys

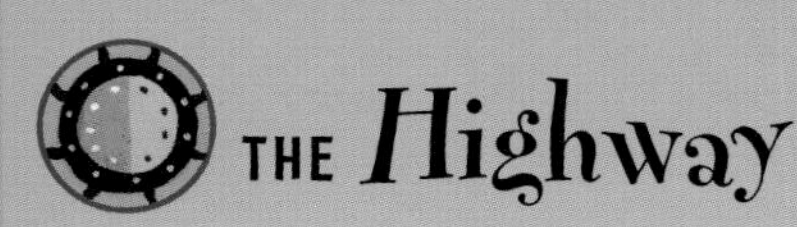

Travel along the *Highway* following a message's journey from its source (the brain) to its end (the people).

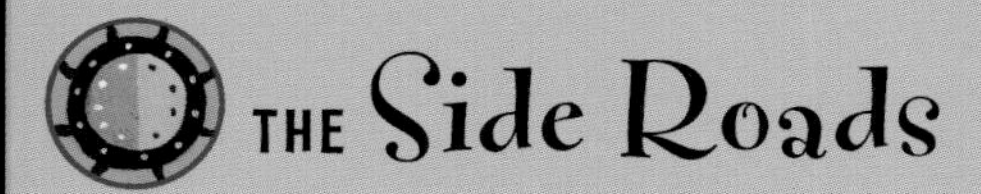

On your journey, you will be asked to select your own route. Choose a *Side Road* and follow its route.

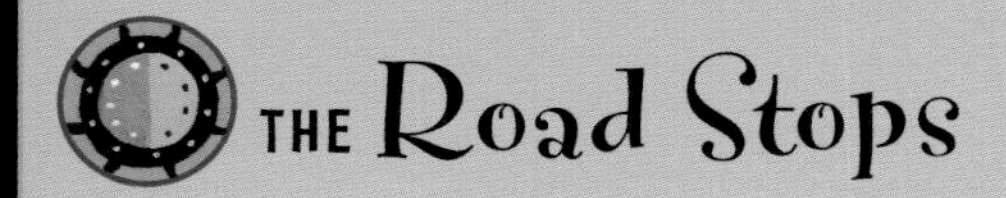

The *Side Roads* lead you to *Road Stops*, which contain vital information about your trip. These may lead you farther to the *Points of Interest*, which are bursting with fascinating facts. *Visible Proof Spots* will test your knowledge with experiments and puzzles. *Detours* allow you to leap forward to *Road Stops* farther along the route. They have a symbol that looks like this. ------------→ Detou

Let's begin our journey!

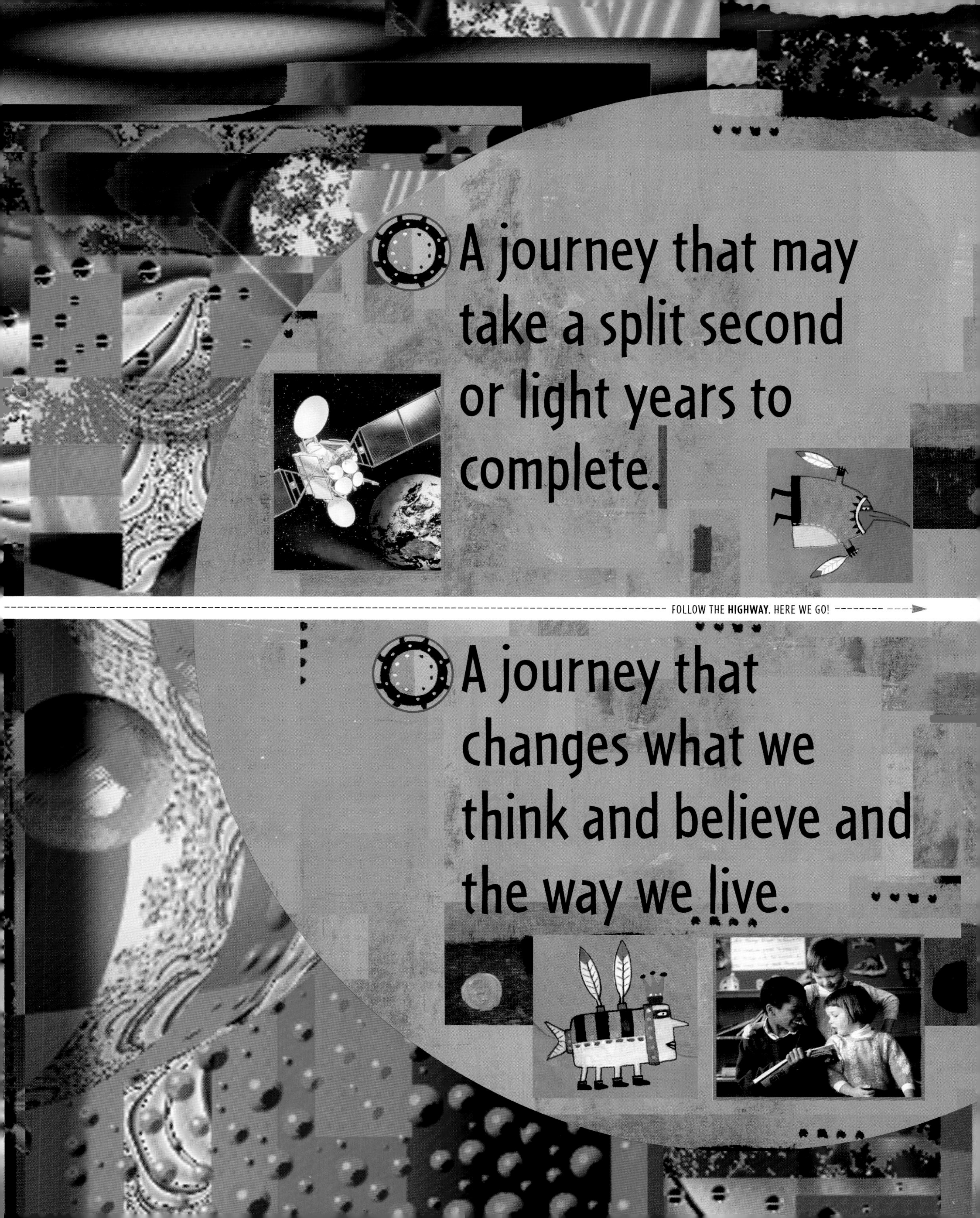

A journey that may take a split second or light years to complete.

FOLLOW THE **HIGHWAY.** HERE WE GO!

A journey that changes what we think and believe and the way we live.

All communication begins in the Brain.

FOLLOW THE **HIGHWAY.**

This is where our journey starts—right in the middle of the human brain.

The brain is the most complex organ in the body. Let's take a look at it.

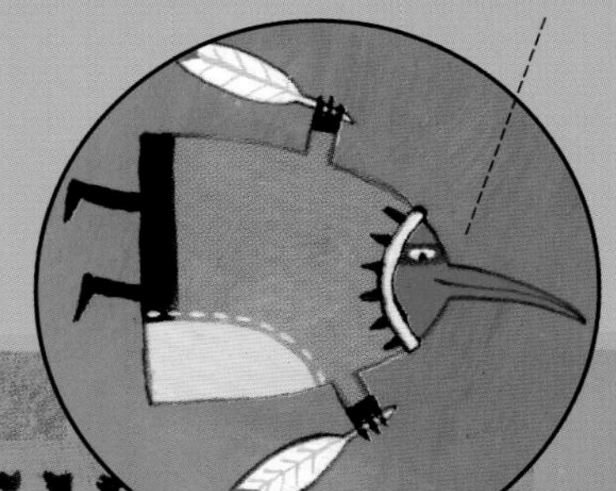

Select YOUR SIDE ROAD

The Brain

Imagine!

Nerve impulses in the brain can travel 180 miles (290 kilometers) per hour—as fast as some racing cars!

ROAD STOP

1 What is the brain?

The brain is the most powerful and complicated organ in the human body. It is the body's control center. The brain floats in a fluid inside the head and is protected by layers of skin called meninges and the thick bones of the skull called the cranium. A network of blood vessels supplies the brain with oxygen.

Detour

DO ALL LIVING CREATURES HAVE BRAINS? FIND OUT IN **ROAD STOP** 3.

What's inside the brain?
The brain is made up of billions of cells. There are two kinds of cells.

1 **NERVE CELLS** (CALLED NEURONS) The electrical and chemical signals that pass from one neuron to the next are responsible for everything we do, feel, and think. The human brain has from 10 billion to 100 billion neurons, which are all connected. One tiny neuron is linked to thousands of others.

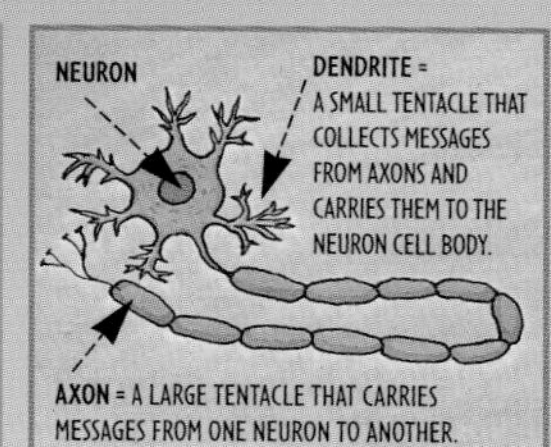
NEURON
DENDRITE = A SMALL TENTACLE THAT COLLECTS MESSAGES FROM AXONS AND CARRIES THEM TO THE NEURON CELL BODY.
AXON = A LARGE TENTACLE THAT CARRIES MESSAGES FROM ONE NEURON TO ANOTHER.

2 **SUPPORTING CELLS** (CALLED GLIA) Although the glia cannot send signals, they are very important because they protect the neurons and keep the brain free from disease.

Visible Proof SPOT

Stack a row of dominoes closely in front of each other. When you knock the first domino down, it causes the rest to topple, one by one. Signals are passed between neurons in a similar way. Electrical pulses are fired off one after another down the axon until they reach the next neuron.

JUST WHY IS THE BRAIN SO IMPORTANT? FOLLOW THIS ROUTE TO ITS POINT OF INTEREST.

FOLLOW THE **HIGHWAY** TO FIND OUT ABOUT THE MESSAGES WE SEND.

POINT of Interest

This organ controls the human body.

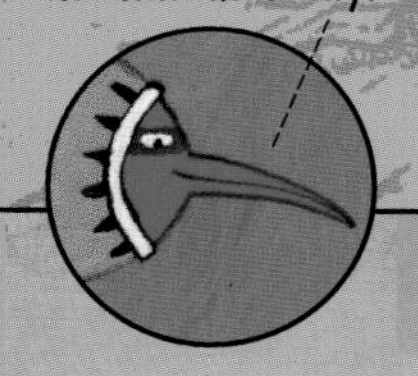

And what does the brain do?

The brain receives information about what is going on inside and outside the body. It then analyzes this information and sends messages out to parts of the body, causing them to act in a certain way.

LOOKING AT BRAINWAVES

Even when you are asleep, the brain is still active, keeping the body alive. Doctors can use an electroencephalograph (EEG) to record the electrical activity, or brain waves, in a person's brain. The EEG patterns show what is happening when the person is awake or asleep.

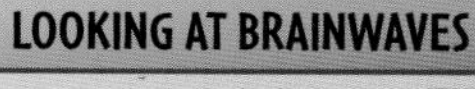
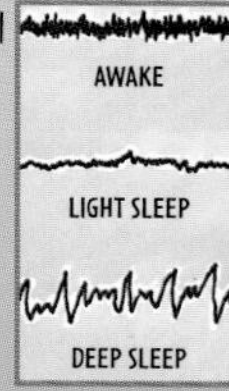
AWAKE
LIGHT SLEEP
DEEP SLEEP

1 The brain controls our behavior.

2 The brain allows us to move.

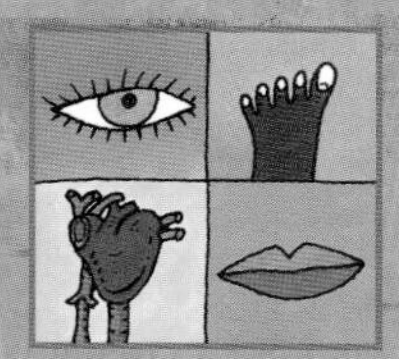

3 The brain makes all the different parts of the body work.

4 The brain stores information from our past, helping us learn and remember.

5 The brain allows us to think and feel.

6 The brain enables us to use language to communicate.

Detour

TO FIND OUT EXACTLY HOW THE BRAIN DOES ALL THIS, TURN TO **ROAD STOP** 4.

HOW BIG IS THE BRAIN? FOLLOW THE **SIDE ROAD** TO ROAD STOP 2.
WHERE DID THE BRAIN COME FROM? FOLLOW THE **SIDE ROAD** TO ROAD STOP 3.
WHAT MAKES THE BRAIN WORK? FOLLOW THE **SIDE ROAD** TO ROAD STOP 4.

ROAD STOP

2 What does the brain look like?

SIDE ROAD TO ROAD STOP 2

The human brain is like a ball of jelly, with grooves and ridges covering its surface. It is grayish pink in color.

THE THREE PARTS OF THE BRAIN

[1] **THE CEREBRUM** This is made up of neurons and glia.
※ It is the largest part of the brain, making up more than three-quarters of the total weight. It has many folds and grooves.
※ A fissure (a large groove) divides the cerebrum into halves, called the left cerebral hemisphere and the right cerebral hemisphere. The outer layer of the cerebrum is called the cortex.
※ Each hemisphere is divided into four regions called lobes.

CROSS-SECTION

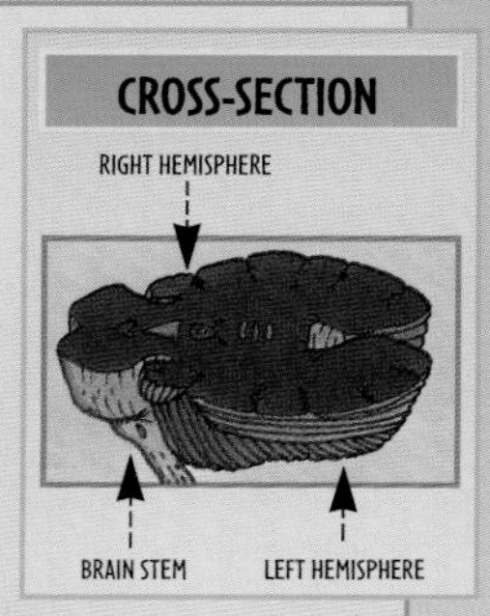

[1] Responsible for intelligence and feelings.

[2] Controls balance, posture, and movement.

[3] Looks after the processes of the body, such as breath

FOLLOW THE **HIGHWAY** AND FIND OUT ABOUT THOUGHT AND IMAGINATION.

ROAD STOP

3 Where did the brain come from

The first living animals were invertebrates—animals without backbones. Invertebrates do not have well-developed brains. Instead, their bodies are controlled by clusters of nerve cells called ganglia. Scientists believe that the human brain developed gradually, or evolved, from ganglia.

THE GROWTH OF THE BRAIN BEFORE A CHILD IS BORN

[1] Every person starts as a single cell. This cell divides and multiplies.

[2] As each cell is forme it takes on a special task becoming part of the bo such as a skin cell.

[3] The first recognizab shape is the central nerv system, made up of the brain and the spinal cor

[4] The rest of the body forms around the centr nervous system.

WHAT ARE THE THREE PARTS OF THE BRAIN? FOLLOW THE **SIDE ROAD** TO ROAD STOP 2.

SIDE ROAD TO ROAD STOP 3

SIDE ROAD TO ROAD STOP 4

] THE CEREBELLUM

is is made up of closely-
cked bundles of nerve cells
lled folia. It has a right and a
ft hemisphere, which link the
fferent sides of the cerebrum
the rest of the body.

] THE BRAIN STEM

is is like a long stalk. It
nnects the cerebrum with
e spinal cord. The bottom
art of the brain stem, or
edulla, controls the body's
tal processes, such as the
eartbeat and breathing.

LLOW THIS ROUTE TO ITS **POINT OF INTEREST**
FIND OUT ABOUT THE BRAIN'S SIZE.

POINT of Interest

Is the brain always the same size?

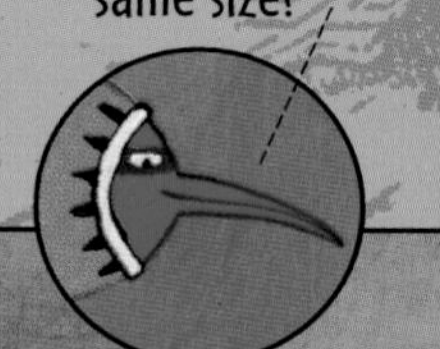

How big is the brain?

The average weight of an adult human brain is about 3 pounds (1.4 kilograms).

COMPARING BRAIN SIZES

NEWBORN'S BRAIN IS LESS THAN 1 POUND (0.5 KG)

SIX-YEAR-OLD BRAIN AT ITS FULL WEIGHT OF 3 POUNDS (1.4 KG)

The brain becomes heavier because the neurons grow in size as you grow. The number of connections between the neurons also increases–axons grow new branches, which link up with the tentaclelike dendrites. The greater the number of connections, the more complex your thinking can be.

Detour

TO FIND OUT MORE ABOUT THE DIFFERENCES BETWEEN THE RIGHT AND LEFT HEMISPHERES, GO TO **ROAD STOP 4**.

Visible Proof SPOT

Clench both of your hands into fists and put them together. That's about the size of your brain!

AND WHAT DOES IT FEEL LIKE?

SMOOTH AND SPRINGY, LIKE GELATIN!

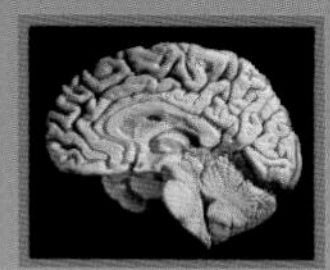

Detour

FIND OUT MORE ABOUT THOUGHT IN **ROAD STOP 6**.

FOLLOW THE **HIGHWAY**. ----►

THE BRAIN AT BIRTH

ewborn baby's brain has up to 100
ion neurons. At the start, most of
neurons are not connected. But
he child grows older and gains new
eriences, connections are made–
broken–between the cells, and
brain develops and grows. When
rons die, they are not replaced.

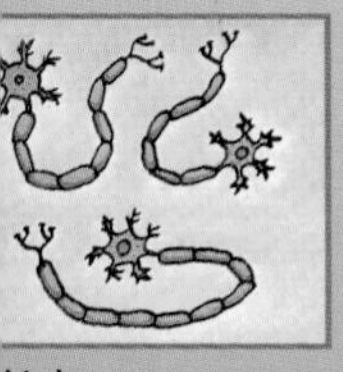

birth, neurons are
y spaced.

※ As learning takes place, neurons form links.

LOW THIS ROUTE TO ITS **POINT OF INTEREST**
DISCOVER IF EVERY ANIMAL HAS A BRAIN.

POINT of Interest

Are all animal brains the same?

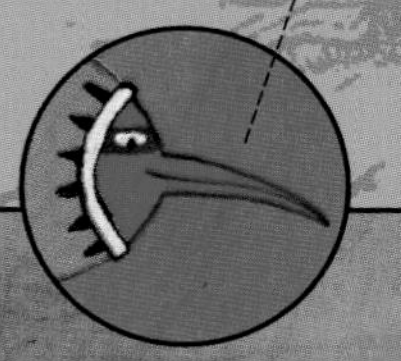

Does every living creature have a brain?

Simple animals, such as worms and insects, have brains made up of just a few groups of nerve cells. Animals with backbones (vertebrates) have complicated brains.

Detour

FIND OUT HOW THE SIZE OF THE BRAIN AFFECTS THE INTELLIGENCE OF A CREATURE IN **ROAD STOP 7**.

1 Sharks and fish have simple brains.

2 Birds and reptiles have a larger cerebrum.

3 Mammals have the most well-developed brains.

MADE TO MEASURE

In some animals, parts of the brain may be particularly developed to give them special skills that help them survive.

※ Birds and fish that migrate are able to navigate their way across vast distances.

※ A dog's sense of smell may be a million times more acute than a human's.

CAN THE BRAIN STOP WORKING PROPERLY? **SIDE ROAD** TO ROAD STOP 4 ---►

ROAD STOP

How does the brain work?

All our actions, thoughts, and ideas are controlled by the brain. The billions of neurons in the brain pass messages, in the form of electrical impulses, between them and then around the body through the nervous system.

Different areas of the brain receive information from such sense organs as the eyes and ears. The brain acts on this information by sending messages to the muscles, organs and other parts of the body.

WHAT HAPPENS WHEN THE BRAIN GOES WRONG? FOLLOW THE PATH TO THE **POINT OF INTEREST**.

SENDING A MESSAGE FROM ONE NEURON TO ANOTHER

1. The message is carried away from the cell body of the neuron along the axon. Messages can travel along nerves at speeds of up to 300 feet (90 meters) per second!
2. Neurons do not quite touch one another. When the message reaches the end of the axon, it has to cross a tiny gap, called a synapse, between the axon and a dendrite of the next cell.
3. Electrical impulses cannot cross the synapse but chemical impulses can. So, the message triggers knobs on the end of the axon into releasing a special chemical called a neurotransmitter. The neurotransmitter bridges the synaptic gap.
4. When enough neurotransmitter has built up at the dendrite, it fires an electrical impulse of its own and the message continues its journey.

RESPONDING TO THE SIGNAL

Each part of the brain is responsible for differen actions. These various control centers decode the message and then instruct the body what to do.

HEARING, SMELLIN, TALKING, MOVING, SEEING, TOUCHIN, UNDERSTANDING, THINKIN

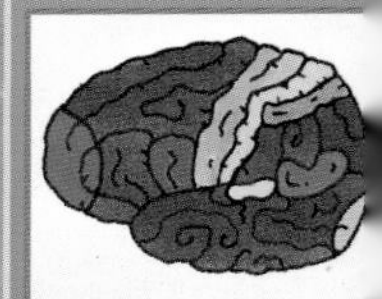

FOLLOW THE **HIGHWAY** AND FIND OUT WHAT MAKES US THINK.

POINT of Interest

What makes the brain not work properly?

Can the brain stop working properly?

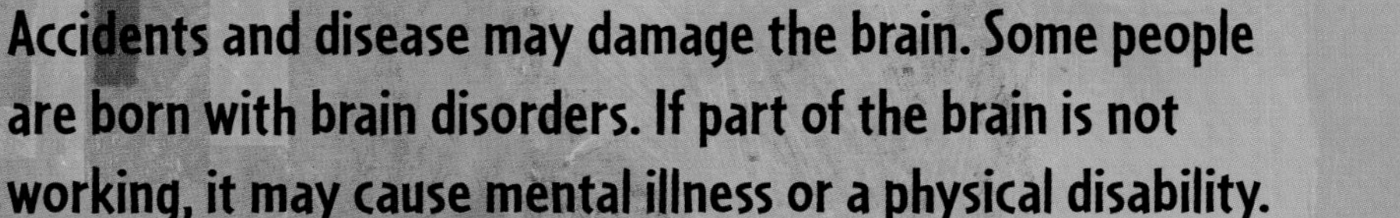

Accidents and disease may damage the brain. Some people are born with brain disorders. If part of the brain is not working, it may cause mental illness or a physical disability.

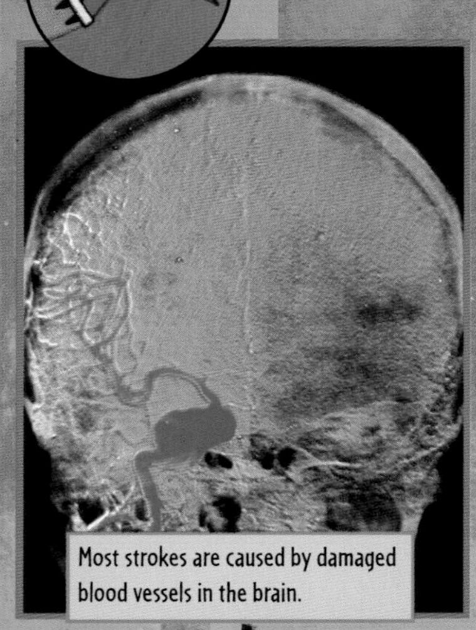

Most strokes are caused by damaged blood vessels in the brain.

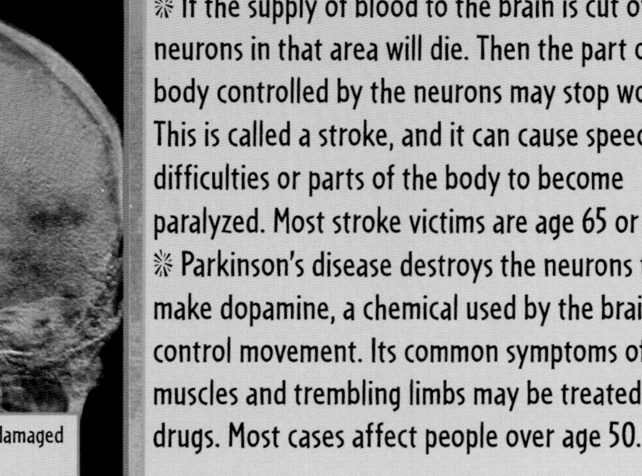

- If the supply of blood to the brain is cut off, neurons in that area will die. Then the part of the body controlled by the neurons may stop working. This is called a stroke, and it can cause speech difficulties or parts of the body to become paralyzed. Most stroke victims are age 65 or older.
- Parkinson's disease destroys the neurons that make dopamine, a chemical used by the brain to control movement. Its common symptoms of stiff muscles and trembling limbs may be treated by drugs. Most cases affect people over age 50.

Visible Proof SPOT

Our brain stores pictures in its memory. The brain will recognize a picture even if you only see a small part of it, or if you only see a hazy outline. Who is this famous person?

ANSWER: MICHAEL JACKSON.

HOW DOES THE BRAIN CARRY OUT ITS TASKS? FOLLOW THE **SIDE ROAD** TO ROAD STOP 4.

THE RIGHT AND LEFT HEMISPHERES

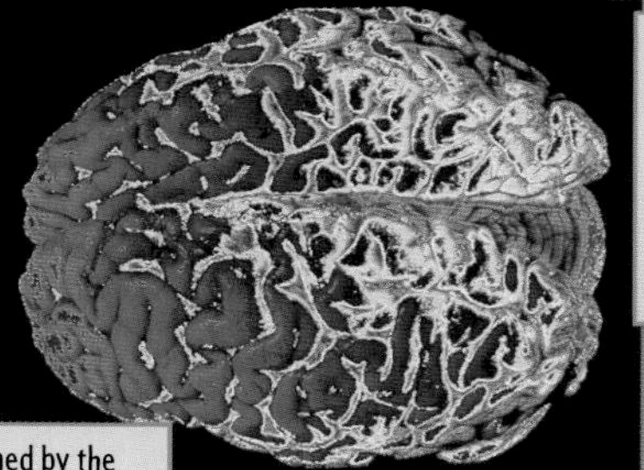

HE LEFT CEREBRAL EMISPHERE controls ie right side of the ody. It is used for eech, language, and ctions that need der and logic.

THE RIGHT CEREBRAL HEMISPHERE controls the left side of the body. It is used for creative thinking and imagination.

he hemispheres are joined by the **ORPUS CALLOSUM**, which allows us use both hemispheres at the same me. This means, for example, that e can read a word and visualize the bject at the same time.

Visible Proof SPOT

To use the left side of your brain, figure out which number comes next: 3, 3, 5, 4, 4, 3, 5, 5, 4, ? To use the right side of your brain, play a musical instrument or draw a picture!

ANSWER: 3 – THE NUMBER OF LETTERS IN THE WORDS 'ONE,' 'TWO,' 'THREE,' ETC.

Detour

FIND OUT MORE ABOUT IMAGINATION IN **ROAD STOP 9**.

Let's examine how we go about making a message.

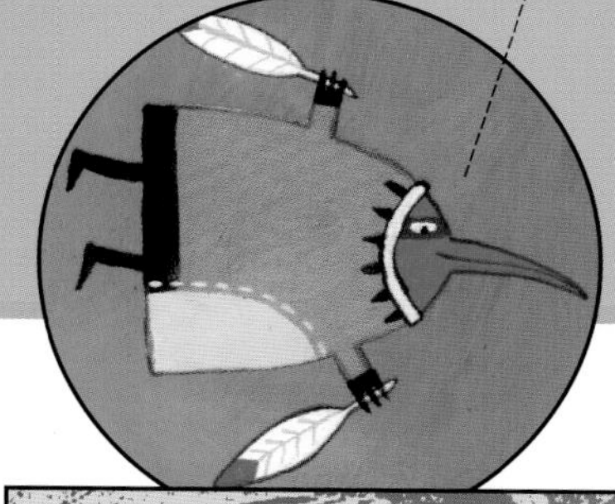

Select
YOUR SIDE ROAD

Messages

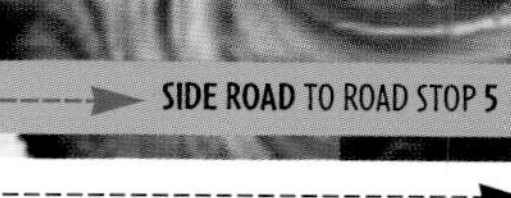

FINDING OUT MORE

There are many areas of the human mind that people do not understand. Scientists study the brain to try to find out more. Neurologists study neurons and the nervous system.

- **CRANIOLOGISTS** study the shape and size of the skull.
- **PSYCHOLOGISTS** study people's behavior.
- **PSYCHIATRISTS** study brain illnesses and disorders.

KEEPING THE BRAIN ALIVE

- The brain needs a constant supply of oxygen to keep it working.
- The brain needs energy from food. When the body has broken down food into glucose, the glucose passes through the bloodstream to the brain.
- A fifth of the body's blood and oxygen supplies are needed for the brain, yet the brain takes up just 2 percent of the body's total weight.

In his book *The Man who Mistook his Wife for a Hat*, the American doctor Oliver Sacks (right) wrote of many rare cases of brain disorder. In one case, a man found that when he looked at faces, he could only make out separate features. He could not put the features together to recognize who the person was–not even his own wife! The part of his brain that controlled visual information contained damaged neurons.

Be Creative!

Some people use their imagination to describe the world in a new way.

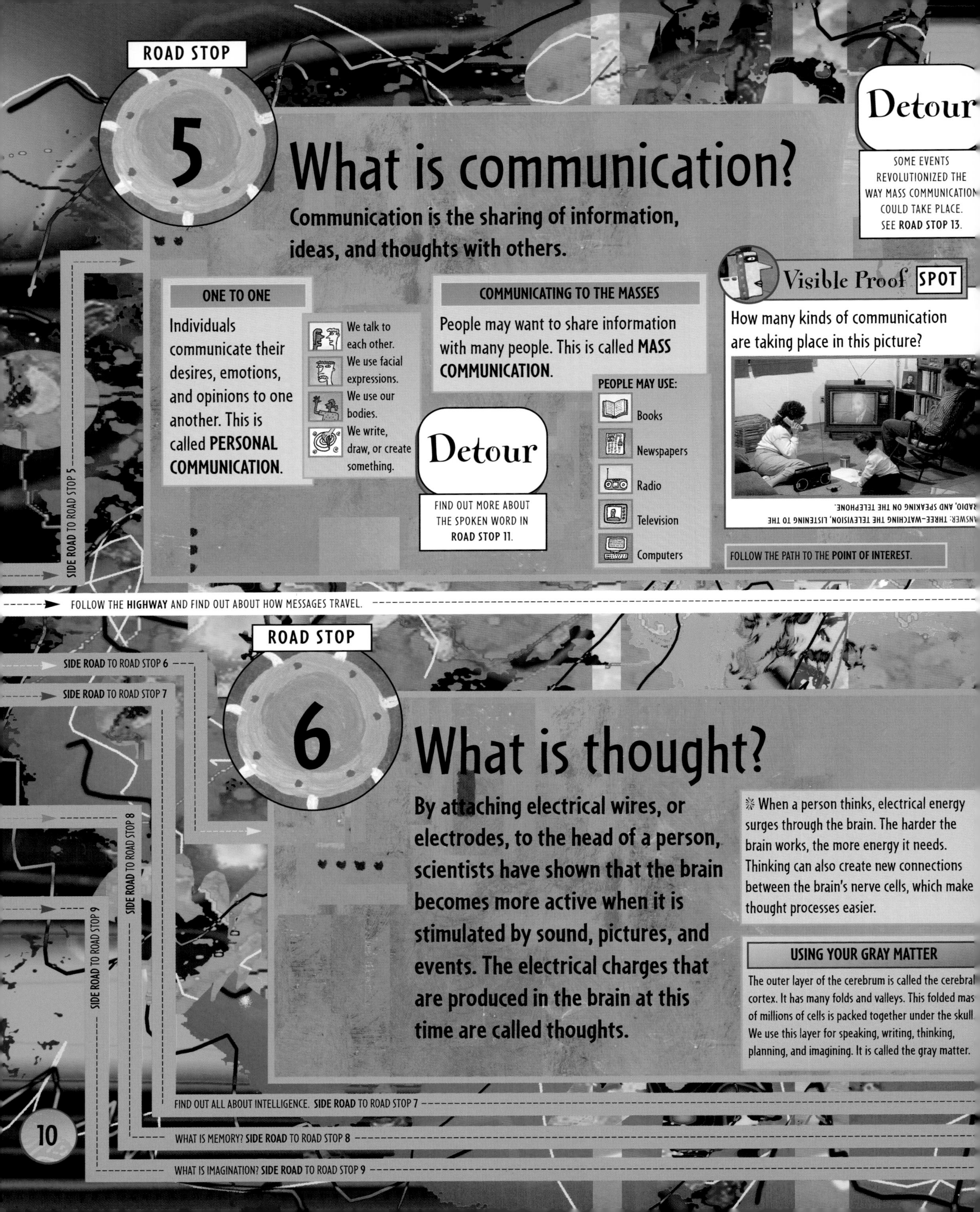

ROAD STOP

5 What is communication?

Communication is the sharing of information, ideas, and thoughts with others.

Detour

SOME EVENTS REVOLUTIONIZED THE WAY MASS COMMUNICATION COULD TAKE PLACE. SEE **ROAD STOP 13**.

ONE TO ONE

Individuals communicate their desires, emotions, and opinions to one another. This is called **PERSONAL COMMUNICATION**.

- We talk to each other.
- We use facial expressions.
- We use our bodies.
- We write, draw, or create something.

Detour

FIND OUT MORE ABOUT THE SPOKEN WORD IN **ROAD STOP 11**.

COMMUNICATING TO THE MASSES

People may want to share information with many people. This is called **MASS COMMUNICATION**.

PEOPLE MAY USE:

- Books
- Newspapers
- Radio
- Television
- Computers

Visible Proof SPOT

How many kinds of communication are taking place in this picture?

ANSWER: THREE—WATCHING THE TELEVISION, LISTENING TO THE RADIO, AND SPEAKING ON THE TELEPHONE.

FOLLOW THE PATH TO THE **POINT OF INTEREST**.

SIDE ROAD TO ROAD STOP 5

FOLLOW THE **HIGHWAY** AND FIND OUT ABOUT HOW MESSAGES TRAVEL.

ROAD STOP

SIDE ROAD TO ROAD STOP 6

SIDE ROAD TO ROAD STOP 7

SIDE ROAD TO ROAD STOP 8

SIDE ROAD TO ROAD STOP 9

6 What is thought?

By attaching electrical wires, or electrodes, to the head of a person, scientists have shown that the brain becomes more active when it is stimulated by sound, pictures, and events. The electrical charges that are produced in the brain at this time are called thoughts.

When a person thinks, electrical energy surges through the brain. The harder the brain works, the more energy it needs. Thinking can also create new connections between the brain's nerve cells, which make thought processes easier.

USING YOUR GRAY MATTER

The outer layer of the cerebrum is called the cerebral cortex. It has many folds and valleys. This folded mass of millions of cells is packed together under the skull. We use this layer for speaking, writing, thinking, planning, and imagining. It is called the gray matter.

FIND OUT ALL ABOUT INTELLIGENCE. **SIDE ROAD** TO ROAD STOP 7

WHAT IS MEMORY? **SIDE ROAD** TO ROAD STOP 8

WHAT IS IMAGINATION? **SIDE ROAD** TO ROAD STOP 9

POINT of Interest

It's a question of sharing.

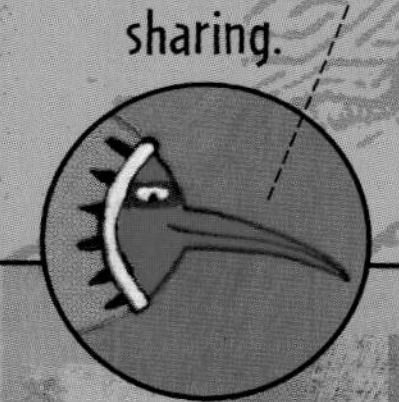

Why is communication important?

We all have feelings and a desire to express the way we feel. Most people are naturally curious. They want to know what is going on in the world around them. By sharing our knowledge and experiences with each other, we learn more about people and about ourselves. Communication lets humans progress and change, or evolve.

Visible Proof SPOT

The message people choose to communicate often depends on their viewpoint. Examine the front pages of two different newspapers reporting the same event. How does each paper present the story? Does it have a certain slant, or bias? What about the headline, or the opening paragraph? What is each paper trying to tell its readers?

Detour

HAVE COMMUNICATION ADVANCES MADE THE WORLD A BETTER PLACE? SEE **ROAD STOP 22**.

FOLLOW THE **HIGHWAY**. ---→

ROAD STOP

7

Why are some people more intelligent than others?

Detour

SOME OF THE MOST INTELLIGENT PEOPLE HAVE SENT MESSAGES THAT HAVE SHAKEN THE WORLD. SEE **ROAD STOP 21**.

There is no link between the size of a person's brain and how clever that person is. Intelligence depends on many things, including the physical nature of the brain, the number and types of connections between the nerve cells, and how a person has been trained to use the brain.

TEST THE BRAIN

An intelligence test measures how clever someone is. A person has to solve problems involving memory, logic, picture sequences, definitions, and calculations. Their score is used to calculate a number known as their intelligence quotient (IQ).

GENE POWER

Every cell in your body contains thousands of instructions called genes. Genes control such characteristics as eye color, nose shape, and hair thickness, and they are passed down through families. Genes are also partly responsible for intelligence.

ENVIRONMENT POWER

What happens to you during your life also determines how clever you are. If information is scarce or you are not encouraged to learn, you may not develop your intelligence to its full power. So, stimulate your brain by reading, discussing, and problem solving!

SIDE ROAD TO ROAD STOP 8 ---→

SIDE ROAD TO ROAD STOP 9 ---→

How do we learn to communicate?

Children learn from an early age to imitate the sounds they hear around them. They also learn to discard those sounds that they are capable of making but that are not used by others.

FOLLOW THIS ROUTE TO THE **POINT OF INTEREST**.

Detour

FIND OUT MORE ABOUT USING CODES IN **ROAD STOP 11**.

Visible Proof SPOT

We learn to communicate by seeing how people around us interact with each other. Do you have an accent? Do you use special words and phrases that only you and your friends understand?

LEARNING TO GET THE MESSAGE ACROSS

2-3 MONTHS: Babies smile and make speechlike sounds.

6 MONTHS: Babies start to develop unique personalities. They choose to do things, such as holding their bottles, in their own way.

12-18 MONTHS: Babies start to imitate older people. They say their first words.

18 MONTHS: A child knows 10 to 20 words and starts to join them together to make phrases.

3 YEARS: A child knows about 900 words.

FOLLOW THE **HIGHWAY** AND FIND OUT HOW WE SEND MESSAGES.

POINT of Interest

What is memory?

How do we remember?

Memories are thought to be formed and stored in an area of the brain called the hippocampus. A memory is formed by repeatedly stimulating the same set of nerve cells, which makes the connections between the cells stronger. If we stop recalling an event, the neurons begin to lose their connections and the memory fades.

EACH PERSON HAS A LONG-TERM AND A SHORT-TERM MEMORY.

LONG-TERM MEMORY
This memory stores all the information we need to know to carry out our daily tasks. Examples include reading, writing, and remembering who we are, what we do, and where we live.

SHORT-TERM MEMORY
Information stays in short-term memory for a few minutes up to a few hours. The information is either discarded, or if recalled often enough, transferred to the long-term memory.

PHOTOGRAPHIC MEMORIES.

Some people have photographic, or eidetic, memories. They can glance at a scene or object and remember every detail. The French emperor Napoleon Bonaparte (1769-1821) could glance at a map and then recall every town and river on it.

Visible Proof SPOT

Play this game to test your friends' memories. Place 20 small objects on a tray and ask your friends to look at the objects for one minute. Then, cover the objects with a cloth. How many items can each person remember?

SIDE ROAD TO ROAD STOP 8

CAN DAYDREAMING BE USEFUL? **SIDE ROAD** TO ROAD STOP 9

ROAD STOP

9 What is imagination?

Imagination is the first stage of creativity. Many people use their imagination to leave the real world behind and create something new. Or they look at old ideas and put them together in a new way.

Detour

WHICH OTHER SCIENTISTS HAVE USED THEIR IMAGINATION TO MAKE THEORIES THAT EXPLAIN THE WORLD? FIND OUT IN **ROAD STOP 21.**

CREATIVE THOUGHTS COME FROM THE RIGHT SIDE OF THE BRAIN.

IMAGINATIVE MESSAGES TO THE WORLD

1 Daydreaming and make-believe can lead to important inventions and discoveries.

ALBERT EINSTEIN (1879-1955)
He put together his famous theory of relativity after daydreaming under a tree and imagining the path of a sunbeam!

2 Artists and writers use their imaginations to show the world in a new way.

VINCENT VAN GOGH (1853-1890)
This Dutch artist created powerful and lively paintings that showed the loneliness and sadness he felt. He suffered a brain disorder that made him violent and depressed. Painting was his way of communicating his feelings to the world.

H. G. WELLS (1866-1946)
This English writer created science-fiction stories in which he imagined how the world might be in the future or how the world could be different today. He wrote about people being invisible or being able to travel through time in time machines.

How does the message travel?

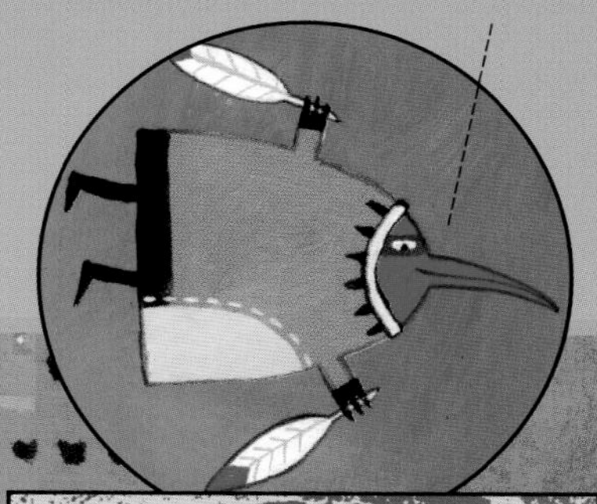

Select

YOUR SIDE ROAD

The Message Travels

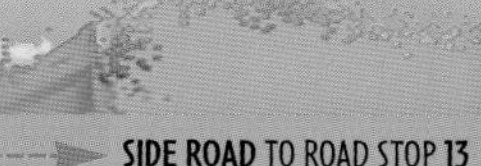

ROAD STOP

10

How were the first messages sen

Nobody knows for sure, but experts believe that prehistoric people probably passed information to each other using grunts and gestures. They may also have imitated the sounds of nature around them, such as the wind rushing through leaves or the cries of animals.

USING PICTURES (20,000 B.C.)

Pictures that represented animals, objects, and events were used to tell stories.

This African cave painting shows a procession of people wearing bushy headdresses.

Detour

WHAT ARE SOME OF THE MOST FAMOUS MESSAGES OF ALL TIME? FIND OUT IN **ROAD STOP 20**.

SIDE ROAD TO ROAD STOP 10

SIDE ROAD TO ROAD STOP 11

FOLLOW THE **HIGHWAY** AND FIND OUT ABOUT WHAT HAPPENS WHEN A MESSAGE ARRIVES AT ITS DESTINATION.

SIDE ROAD TO ROAD STOP 12

ROAD STOP

11

How do we get our message across today?

There are many methods that we can use to relay our message to others, including words, pictures, codes, and even our bodies.

WE USE LANGUAGE

The word language comes from the Latin "lingua," meaning "tongue." Most languages have both a writt and a verbal form. There are about 6,000 languages spoken around the world and thousands more dialec which are local variations of a language.

SIDE ROAD TO ROAD STOP 13
SIDE ROAD TO ROAD STOP 14
SIDE ROAD TO ROAD STOP 15
DIFFERENT COUNTRIES HAVE DIFFERENT WAYS TO SEND MESSAGES. **SIDE ROAD** TO ROAD STOP 12
INVENTIONS AND EVENTS HAVE CHANGED THE WAY WE SEND MESSAGES. **SIDE ROAD** TO ROAD STOP 13
SOME MESSAGES TAKE A LONG TIME GETTING FROM SENDER TO RECEIVER. **SIDE ROAD** TO ROAD STOP 14
SOME MESSAGES ARE BEAUTIFUL TO LOOK AT. **SIDE ROAD** TO ROAD STOP 15

THERE IS EVIDENCE OF OTHER EARLY FORMS OF WRITING: CHINESE (1500 B.C.), GREEK (1400 B.C.) AND LATIN (500 B.C.).

USING PICTURES TO REPRESENT WORDS (3000 B.C.)

The earliest known form of writing that could convey complicated messages was developed by the Sumerians in what is now southeastern Iraq. It is called cuneiform. People made cuneiform symbols on wet clay tablets. The clay was then left out in the sun until it hardened.

Visible Proof SPOT

Cuneiform symbols began as simple pictures. Look at these original symbols. Can you guess what they represented?

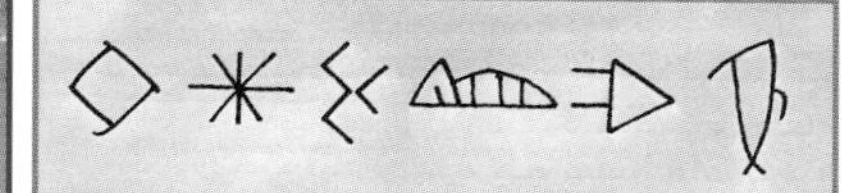

ANSWERS (L-R): THE SUN, GOD OR HEAVEN, MOUNTAIN, MAN, OX, FISH.

Gradually, the symbols were simplified into short, wedge-shaped strokes:

HIEROGLYPHICS (3000 B.C.)

The ancient Egyptians sent messages using picturelike signs called hieroglyphics to represent words. The word "hieroglyphic" means "sacred carving."

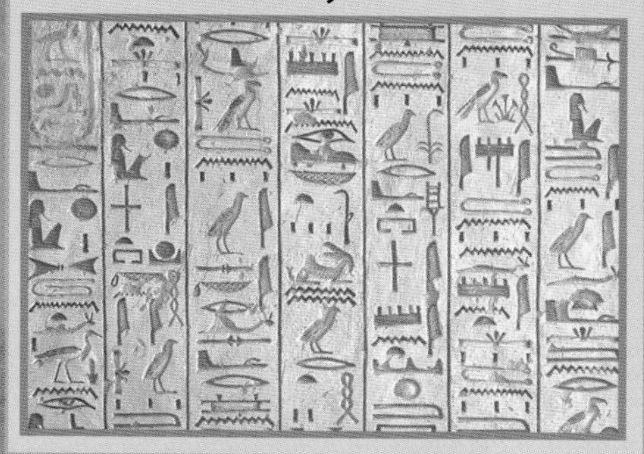

FOLLOW THE **HIGHWAY.**

HE SPOKEN WORD We use conversation when e speaking face-to-face or by telephone. Some ages are only spoken by a few thousand people. s are spoken by hundreds of millions.

most widely spoken languages in the world are:
andarin Chinese = 825 million
nglish = 431 million
indi = 325 million
panish = 320 million
ussian = 187 million
engali = 178 million
panese = 124 million

f people use their hands to communicate with h other. This is called sign language. There are s for many different words, and there is also a -language alphabet.

2 THE WRITTEN WORD Rather than using pictures to represent objects, symbols were created to represent sounds. An early alphabet was developed by the Phoenicians about 1000 B.C. We still use some of their characters in the English alphabet today.

A blind Frenchman called Louis Braille (1809-1852) was only 15 years old when he started to improve the system of writing for the blind. In his Braille alphabet, each letter is represented by a raised pattern of dots that are read with the fingertips.

Not everyone can read and write. In the United States, more than 97 percent of people can read and write, compared to 18 percent in Burkina Faso, West Africa.

WE USE CODES Codes help us to communicate in situations when we cannot speak or write to each other.

1 MORSE CODE Before the invention of the telephone, the quickest way of sending long-distance messages was by telegraph. Messages traveled along wires as electric signals. An American, Samuel Morse (1791-1872), developed one of the first telegraphs and used a code of short and long sounds.

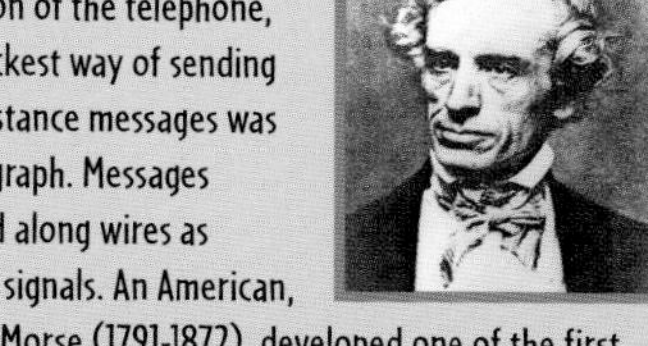

2 SEMAPHORE If ships at sea do not have radio contact, they may use a code called semaphore, which was invented in 1860. Messages are spelled out with two flags in particular positions to represent letters of the alphabet.

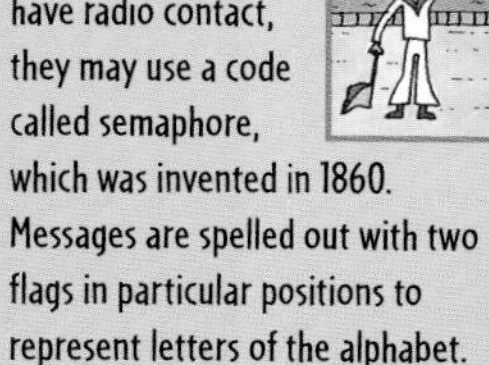

WE USE OUR BODIES People use their faces and bodies to convey messages. This is called body language. The human face has 30 muscles which can be used to create different expressions.

SIDE ROAD TO ROAD STOP 12
SIDE ROAD TO ROAD STOP 13
SIDE ROAD TO ROAD STOP 14
SIDE ROAD TO ROAD STOP 15

ROAD STOP

12 How and when do we send messages?

How you send a message depends on the technology available to the sender of the message and the receiver, on circumstance, and on the impact you want to make.

Detou[r]

LEAP TO **ROAD STOP 1**[…] FIND OUT MORE ABO[…] COMMUNICATING B[…] COMPUTER.

SOME PEOPLE HAVE MORE CHOICES THAN OTHERS. **SIDE ROAD** TO ROAD STOP 12

1 Using what is available

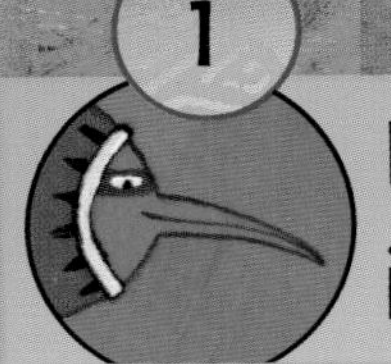

Throughout the world, people have access to different machines and tools. Some can choose from many communication methods. Others have a more limited choice.

So, if you have something to tell someone, what do you do? Here are some choices.

POST

The first mail boxes were erected in Britain in 1853. Before the introduction of stamps, the cost of mailing a letter was paid by the person receiving it.

TELEPHONE

Alexander Graham Bell (1847-1922), (right) an American inventor and educator, patented the telephone in 1876. Telephones work by changing the voice's sound waves into an electric current, transmitting it down a network of wires, and then changing it back into sound waves.

FOLLOW THE **HIGHWAY** AND FIND OUT HOW THE WAY WE COMMUNICATE HAS AFFECTED OUR LANDSCAPE.

2 A question of circumstance

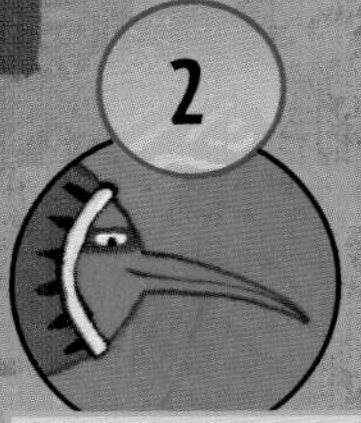

Not everybody has the same choices. Some groups of people live in small, and sometimes isolated, communities and have developed their own unique methods of communication.

3 Making an impact

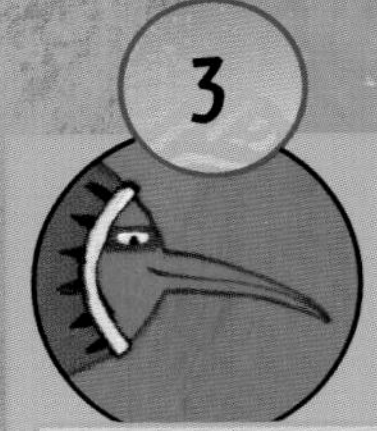

ADVERTISEMENTS

Ads are messages that are specially designed to sell or promote a product or an idea. Advertising is used by individuals, groups, and governments to communicate ideas about themselves to other people. The content and look of an advertisement will depend on the kind of image the advertiser wants to reflect.

Visible Proof SPOT

What is this advertisement trying to tell you about the product being sold? Do you believe the message?

ANSWER: DRINKING THE PRODUCT WILL MAKE YOUR LIFE MUCH HAPPIER.

SIDE ROAD TO ROAD STOP 12

CERTAIN EVENTS HAVE CHANGED THE WAY WE COMMUNICATE. **SIDE ROAD** TO ROAD STOP 13

HOW HAS THE TIME NEEDED TO SEND A MESSAGE BEEN REDUCED? **SIDE ROAD** TO ROAD STOP 14

SOME MESSAGES ARE SENT IN A SIMPLE FORM, OTHERS ARE MORE ELABORATE. **SIDE ROAD** TO ROAD STOP 15

E-MAIL

ıe first personal computer
°C) was the Altair, produced
the United States in 1975.
·day, PC's allow users to
nd messages to each other
ı the screen in seconds via
ectronic mail, or e-mail.

MOBILE TELEPHONE

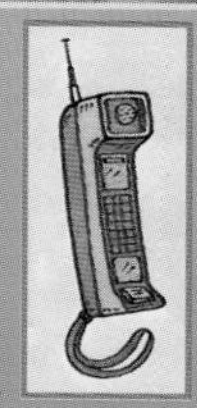

Mobile, or cellular, telephones first appeared in Sweden in the late 1970's. They have no cord or cables and can be used almost anywhere.

FAX

‹ (short for
simile) is
vay of
nsmitting
d receiving
t and
ages over telephone lines.
he 1930's, newspapers first
gan using fax machines to
nsmit photographs.

RADIO

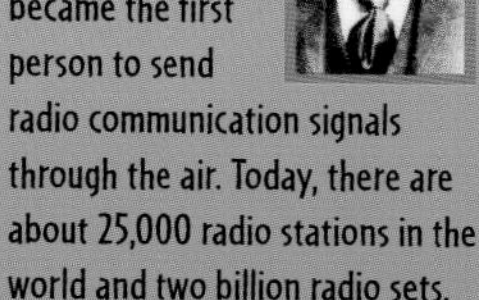

In 1895, the Italian inventor Guglielmo Marconi (1874-1937) became the first person to send radio communication signals through the air. Today, there are about 25,000 radio stations in the world and two billion radio sets.

TELEVISION

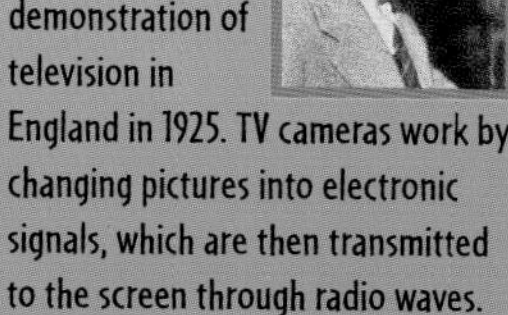

Scottish engineer John Logie Baird (1888-1946) gave the first public demonstration of television in England in 1925. TV cameras work by changing pictures into electronic signals, which are then transmitted to the screen through radio waves.

POINT of Interest

Some strange ways of sending messages!

What other forms of communication have been used?

Throughout history, people have sent messages in all kinds of unusual ways.

WALLS THAT SPELL WORDS

The ancient Greeks used a form of communication that involved lighting fires at various points along the tops of walls. Each part of the wall stood for a different letter of the alphabet. The receiver spelled out words according to where the fires were lit.

FOLLOW THE **HIGHWAY.**

FIRST ADVERTISEMENTS

ʼ000 B.C. Historians believe that the
ylonians, who lived in what is now
, were the first to use advertising.
y hung signs above their shop doors
romote what they were selling.
bols were used to represent the
ds for sale.
500 B.C. In Egypt, merchants paid
rs to announce to passers-by that
cargo ships had arrived.

Detour

LEAP TO **ROAD STOP 13** TO SEE WHICH INVENTIONS ALLOWED PEOPLE TO SEND THEIR MESSAGES MORE QUICKLY.

ART

Art is also a way of communicating ideas. Some artists have tried to express themselves and their ideas by using shapes and color in innovative ways.

Surrealism was an art movement that began in Paris in 1924. Surrealist artists were interested in the mind and dreams. The Spanish painter Joan Miró (1893-1983) used round, curled, and geometric symbols, and bright colors (above). His paintings were full of hidden messages.

FOLLOW THIS ROUTE TO ITS **POINT OF INTEREST.**

MAPS MADE OF STICKS

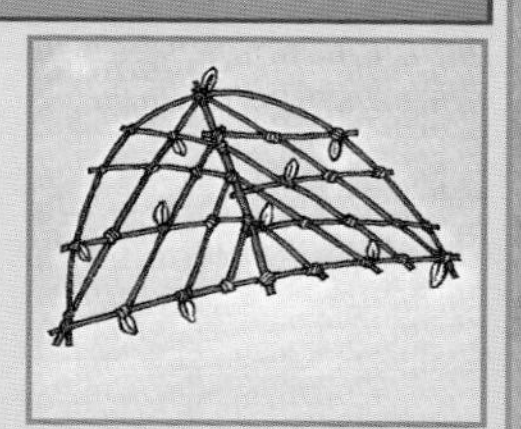

More than 500 years ago, stick maps were used by people in some coastal regions to tell each other where nearby islands were and what the sea currents were like. Small shells marked the islands, and the currents were shown by the curves of the sticks.

MESSAGES IN THE MIND

Extrasensory perception (ESP) is communicating without using the five known senses. Some people claim to be able to receive messages in the form of thoughts directly from the minds of others. Most people doubt ESP exists because there is little scientific proof.

Detour

WHAT WILL THE NEXT ADVANCES IN COMMUNICATION BE? LEAP TO **ROAD STOP** 23.

SIDE ROAD TO ROAD STOP 13
SIDE ROAD TO ROAD STOP 14
SIDE ROAD TO ROAD STOP 15

ROAD STOP

13 What important events revolutionized the way messages were sent?

LEAP TO **ROAD STOP 21** TO SEE HOW BOOKS HAVE BEEN USED TO SPREAD IDEAS AND BELIEFS.

WHAT PAPER IS LIKE DEPENDS ON:
- The kind of pulp used–wood, cotton, linen, and so on.
- The way the pulp is processed.
- The type of machine used to make the sheets of paper.

Some inventions and episodes in history opened up new ways of communicating for millions of people. They include the invention of paper and printing machines, the development of the postal system, and the use of satellites and computers.

FOLLOW THE **HIGHWAY** TO FIND OUT HOW NEW COMMUNICATION METHODS HAVE AFFECTED WHERE PEOPLE LIVE AND WORK.

FIND OUT ABOUT INVENTIONS AND EPISODES THAT CHANGED THE WORLD. **SIDE ROAD** TO ROAD STOP 13

3 The story of the postal system

RELAY TEAMS

- The first postal systems used either runners or couriers on horseback. They were stationed at intervals along roads and passed messages to each other. A string of couriers could carry messages more than 90 miles (150 km) each day.
- The Roman emperor Augustus Caesar built relay stations along the roads. These were resting places for messengers and their horses.

THE POST

- In the 1400's, as the number of people who could read and write grew, more people started to communicate by letter. In Vienna, Austria, the Taxis family employed approximately 20,000 private couriers to work across central Europe.
- In the 1600's, governments across Europe started to set up public postal systems.
- In 1837, a retired British teacher named Rowland Hill suggested a standard postage cost, regardless of the distance. Until then, the cost of mailing a letter depended on how far it had to travel. He also proposed that the sender buy small labels–stamps–to stick on the letter so that the postage was paid for in advance.

MAIL ON THE RAILWAY

In the late 1880's, as train networks developed, the postal system started to use special road cars that picked up mail sacks en route. Postal workers sorted the mail on the train as it moved along.

- **1789** The United States had 75 post offices.
- **1901** This number had increased to 77,000 post offices.
- **1997** There are about 40,000 post offices. Although more messages are sent, people have found other ways of communicating.

Detour

LEAP TO **ROAD STOP 15** TO FIND OUT WHICH ELECTRONIC DEVELOPMENT IS NOW AN ALTERNATIVE TO TRADITIONAL MAIL.

HOW LONG DOES IT TAKE TO SEND A MESSAGE? **SIDE ROAD** TO ROAD STOP 14

WHAT IS E-MAIL? **SIDE ROAD** TO ROAD STOP 15

1

The invention of paper

EGYPTIAN PAPYRUS

In ancient Egypt, papyrus reeds were cut into strips that were then weaved together and pressed into sheets. This textured material was the earliest form of paper and was used for important documents.

CHINESE PULP

Paper as we know it was invented by the Chinese more than 2,000 years ago. It was made by pounding rope, rags, or bark into a pulp and then rolling it into sheets.

MACHINE-MADE PAPER

Until the end of the 1700's, almost all paper was made by hand, sheet by sheet. In 1798, a Frenchman named Nicholas Louis Robert, created a machine that could produce paper in long rolls.

2

The importance of printing machines

1 BLOCK PRINTING The first form of printing was made by the Chinese around A.D. 100. First, they carved pictures and letters on wooden blocks. Then, they put ink on these designs and pressed paper on the inked blocks, transferring the image on the paper.

2 MOVABLE TYPE Around 1045, a Chinese printer, Bi Sheng, invented the first movable type. He made separate clay pieces for each character, or letter. These were then reused.

3 THE PRINTING PRESS
Around 1440, German metalsmith Johannes Gutenberg developed the first printing press to use movable type (right). It was adapted from a machine used to press grapes or cheese.

Visible Proof SPOT

How many printed items do you use everyday? What information do they give you? Examine this list and then make one of your own: books, comics, postcards, posters, advertisements.

HOW DID PRINTING CHANGE THE WORLD?
Printing allowed ideas, facts, and knowledge to be passed to more people, more quickly and more cheaply than before. It encouraged people to learn how to read and write.

Detour

ARE SOME BOOKS SO BEAUTIFUL THAT THEY ARE CONSIDERED WORKS OF ART? LEAP TO **ROAD STOP 15** TO FIND OUT.

FOLLOW THE **HIGHWAY.** →

4

Artificial satellites in space

An artificial satellite is any manufactured object that circles a planet. Communications satellites orbit the Earth and allow people to pass messages from one side of the world to the other relatively quickly. The first artificial satellite, Sputnik 1, was launched by the Soviet Union in 1957. By the early 1990's, about 2,000 satellites were operating in orbit.

HOW DO COMMUNICATIONS SATELLITES WORK?

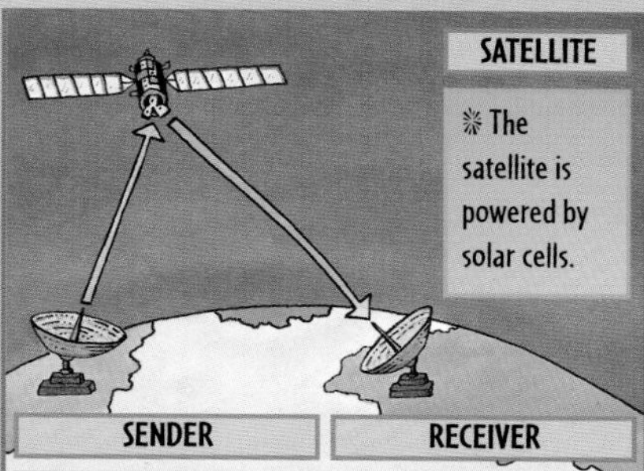

SATELLITE
* The satellite is powered by solar cells.

SENDER
* A telecommunications station has a dish-shaped aerial that points at the satellite. The aerial transmits radio signals to the satellite.

RECEIVER
* The signals are beamed back from the satellite to an aerial in a telecommunications station in another part of the world.

* Each communications satellite can relay television pictures and many telephone calls at the same time.

5

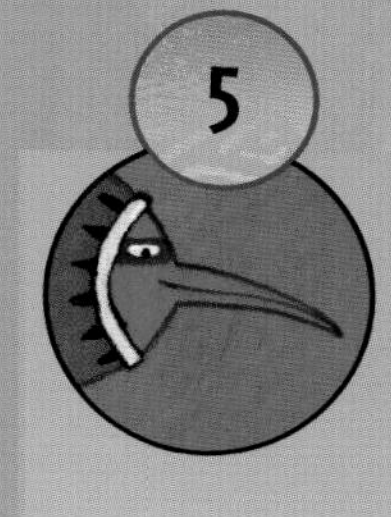

A chip that changed the world

The first computer chip (also called an integrated circuit) was patented in 1959. A chip is the brain of an electronic machine. It may be no bigger than a fingernail, yet it contains all the information needed to make such complicated machines as computers, cameras, and mobile telephones work.

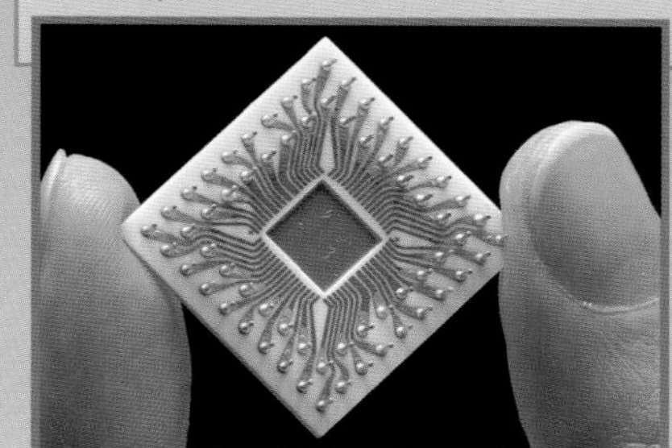

SIDE ROAD TO ROAD STOP 14 →
SIDE ROAD TO ROAD STOP 15 →

ROAD STOP

14

How long does it take to send a message?

That depends on how the message is being sent and where it is going from and to. In the past, messages took much longer to reach their destinations.

SENDING A MESSAGE FROM LONDON TO NEW YORK.

DATE MESSAGE SENT	METHOD OF SENDING MESSAGE	TIME LAPSE BETWEEN SENDING AND RECEIVING MESSAGE
1750	SAILING SHIP	FROM 6 TO 9 WEEKS
1840	FAST SAILING SHIPS CALLED CLIPPERS	ABOUT 12 DAYS
1858	FIRST TRANSATLANTIC TELEGRAPH	SECONDS
1956	FIRST TRANSATLANTIC TELEPHONE CALL	SECONDS
1958	FIRST COMMUNICATIONS SATELLITE	IMMEDIATE
1970	FIRST OVERSEAS DIRECT DIAL PHONE CALL	IMMEDIATE
1990's	COMPUTERS	POTENTIALLY IMMEDIATE

FOLLOW THIS ROUTE TO ITS **POINT OF INTEREST.**

FOLLOW THE **HIGHWAY** TO FIND OUT WHAT IMPACT SOME MESSAGES HAVE HAD ON THE WORLD.

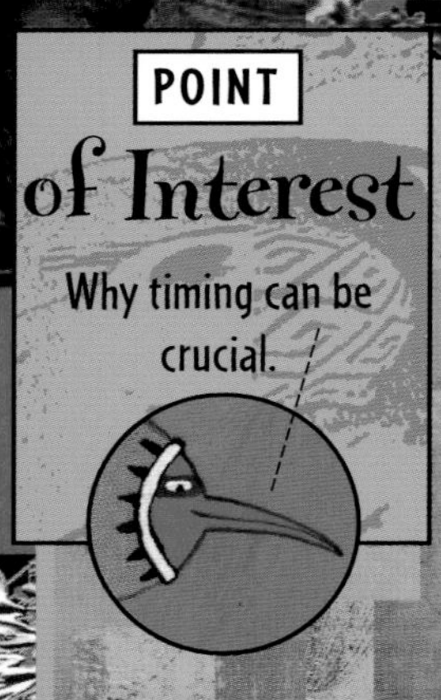

POINT
of Interest
Why timing can be crucial.

And how is it getting quicker and easier to send messages?

Human beings are constantly striving for technological advances. Scientists and inventors seek to improve the links between individuals and between larger groups of people.

HOW DO MOBILE PHONES WORK?

The area covered by a mobile telephone network is divided up into cells. Each cell has a relay station that can receive and transmit signals. When a person makes a call, the mobile phone transmits radio waves to the nearest relay station. This directs it either to a standard telephone network or to another mobile phone user.

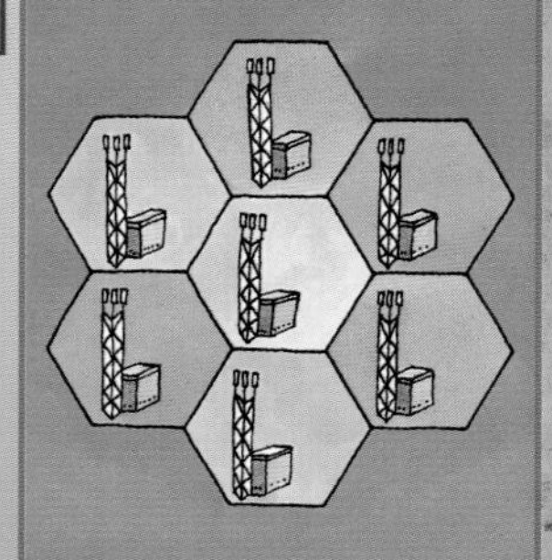

Portable satellite terminals are being developed for people working in isolated areas. These terminals will allow a person to send messages even if the area is not linked to a telecommunications network.

Detou

CAN ADVANCES IN COMMUNICATION TECHNOLOGY HAVE A NEGATIVE EFFECT? TO FIND OUT, LEAP T **ROAD STOP 22.**

WHAT WAS THE INDUSTRIAL REVOLUTION? **SIDE ROAD** TO ROAD STOP 14

SOME PEOPLE LABOR OVER THEIR MESSAGES. OTHERS PRODUCE SOMETHING MORE DISPOSABLE. **SIDE ROAD** TO ROAD STOP 15

Visible Proof SPOT

If you are speaking on the telephone to a friend in another country, there may be a short delay between your friend speaking and you hearing their voice. This time-delay happens because the radio signals that carry the sound sometimes travel long distances up to a satellite and then back down again.

THEN AND NOW...

☀ **Around 1200 B.C.** According to legend, when the Greeks captured the city of Troy, they lit bonfires on hills to tell the people in Argos, nearly 500 miles (800 km) away, that they had won the Trojan War.

☀ **1985** The Live Aid concerts in London and Philadelphia were beamed live across the world by 12 satellites and viewed by about 1.6 billion people. The concerts raised money for starving people in Africa.

A RUSH OF ACTIVITY AND NEW IDEAS

The 1800's was a time when many new machines were invented, and goods and materials became mass-produced. This changed and usually improved the way people communicated. This time in history is known as the Industrial Revolution.

1 TYPEWRITER
This machine was invented in 1867 by three Americans. Writing by hand was no longer the only way to send a written message.

2 PHONOGRAPH
The phonograph was created in 1877 by the American inventor Thomas Edison (1847-1931). It recorded sound by a needle vibrating against a cylinder wrapped in foil.

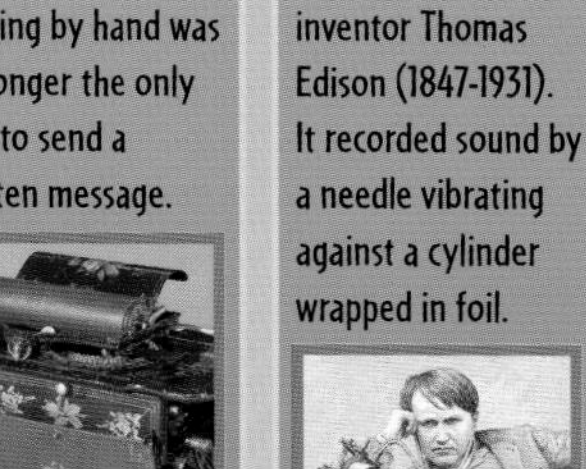

3 RADIO
In 1895, Guglielmo Marconi sent the first telegraph signals through the air rather than along wires.

Detour

WHAT EFFECT DID THE INDUSTRIAL REVOLUTION HAVE ON WHERE PEOPLE LIVED? LEAP TO **ROAD STOP 17**.

FOLLOW THE **HIGHWAY**. →

WHAT IS THE INTERNET?

network is a set of computers that are linked gether so that people can pass information from e computer terminal to another. The Internet, or et," is a massive network made up of thousands smaller computer networks, which are connected the international telephone system.

WHO INVENTED THE INTERNET?
The Internet was created in the late 1960's, when the U.S. Department of Defense connected military and government computers. This complicated network was designed so that if some of the computers were destroyed in a war, messages could still get through the undamaged links. Soon, universities, businesses, and individuals were allowed to add their computers to the network. By the year 2000, an estimated 750 million people will be linked to the Internet.

THE IMPORTANCE OF GETTING THE RIGHT MESSAGE ACROSS

Getting the right message to the right person at the right time may be crucial. The war of 1812 between Britain and the United States should never have happened. On June 18, the United States declared war on Britain for interfering with U.S. shipping. Britain had, in fact, decided to stop interfering with U.S. ships two days before. But by the time the message had traveled across the Atlantic Ocean by ship, the war had begun.

Detour

WHAT IS ELECTRONIC MAIL? LEAP TO **ROAD STOP 15** TO FIND OUT.

SIDE ROAD TO ROAD STOP 15 →

ROAD STOP

15

How does the speed at which messages are made affect how long they will last?

Before the invention of the printing press, books had to be copied by hand by scribes. One book could take months to complete. Each copy was unique and thought to be precious.

FOLLOW THE **HIGHWAY** TO THE ARRIVAL ZONE.

PRESERVING THE MESSAGE

During the Middle Ages, monks in Europe developed great skills in writing and bookmaking. The manuscripts that they produced have been preserved and admired for hundreds of years. This is because their work was beautiful and rare.

The Book of Kells is an illuminated manuscript of the Gospels. Letters are highly decorated with gold, and borders have brightly colored pictures and patterns. This book was produced between the mid-700's and early 800's at the monastery of Kells in County Meath, Ireland.

DISPOSABLE MESSAGES

Today, networks link computers to each other. This allows users to send electronic mail, or e-mail, from machine to machine. A message typed into the sender's computer passes along the network and is delivered into the receiver's computer. This can take just a few seconds, even if the sender and receiver are thousands of miles apart. Once the message has been received, it is generally discarded to keep the computer's memory free. Important messages may be saved onto a disk or printed out.

We made it from the sender to the receiver—prepare for impact!

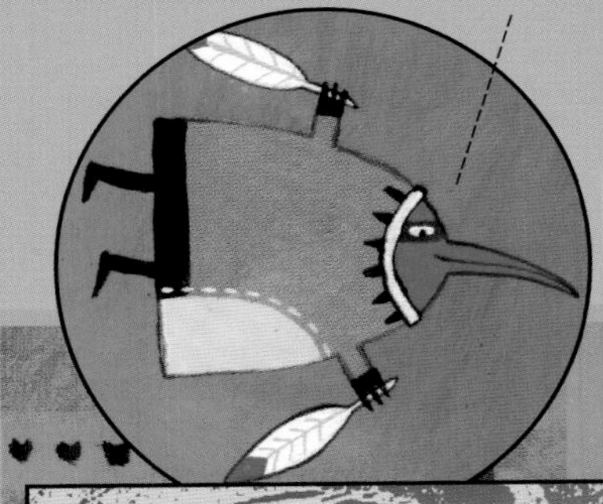

AT DESTINATION

THE MESSAGE REACHES THE

People.

WHAT CAN WE EXPECT TO HAPPEN TO IMPROVE COMMUNICATION IN THE FUTURE? LEAP TO **ROAD STOP 23**.

WHO DECORATED THEIR MESSAGES WITH GOLD? **SIDE ROAD TO ROAD STOP 15**

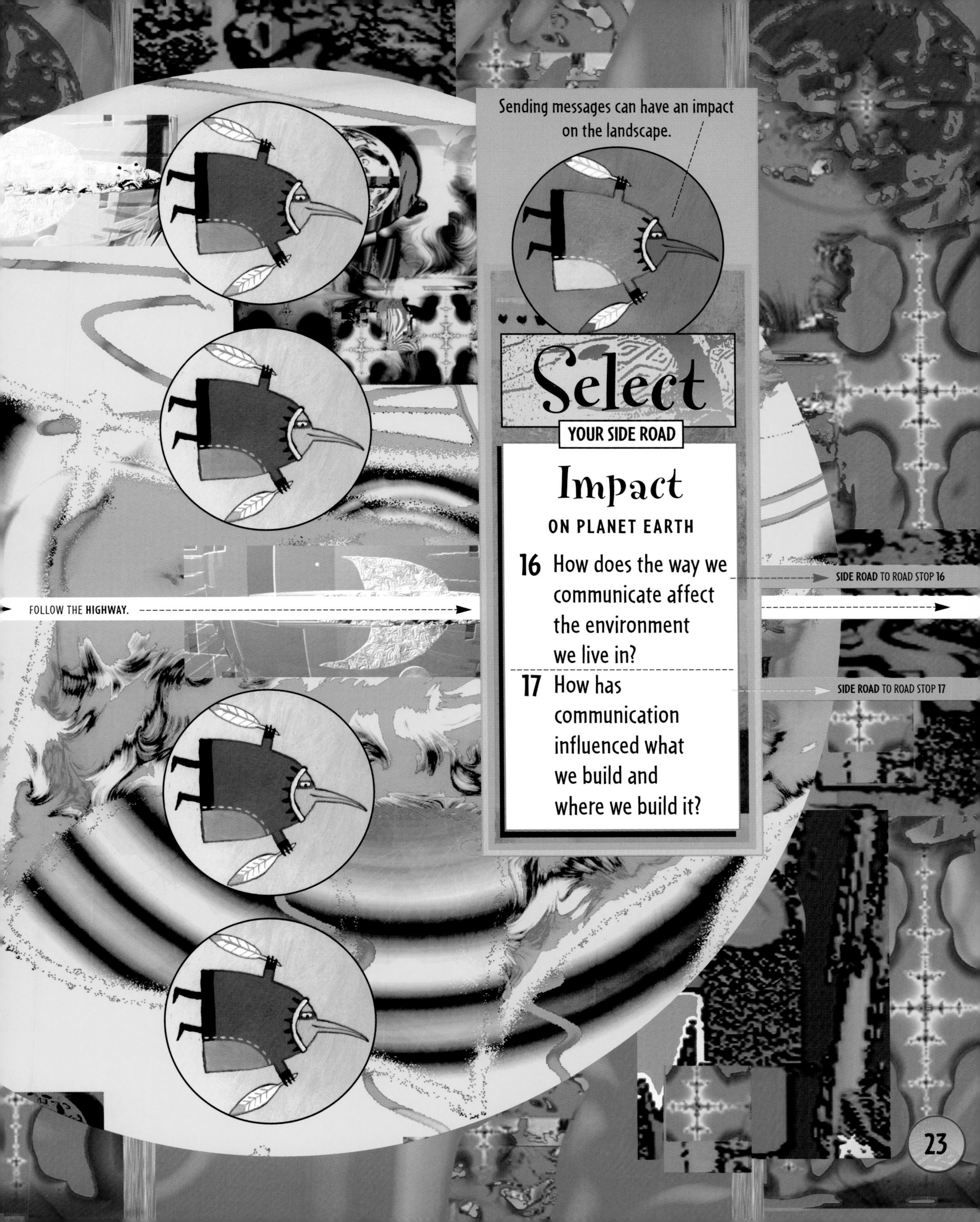
Sending messages can have an impact on the landscape.
Select
YOUR SIDE ROAD
Impact
ON PLANET EARTH
16 How does the way we communicate affect the environment we live in?
SIDE ROAD TO ROAD STOP 16
17 How has communication influenced what we build and where we build it?
SIDE ROAD TO ROAD STOP 17
FOLLOW THE HIGHWAY.

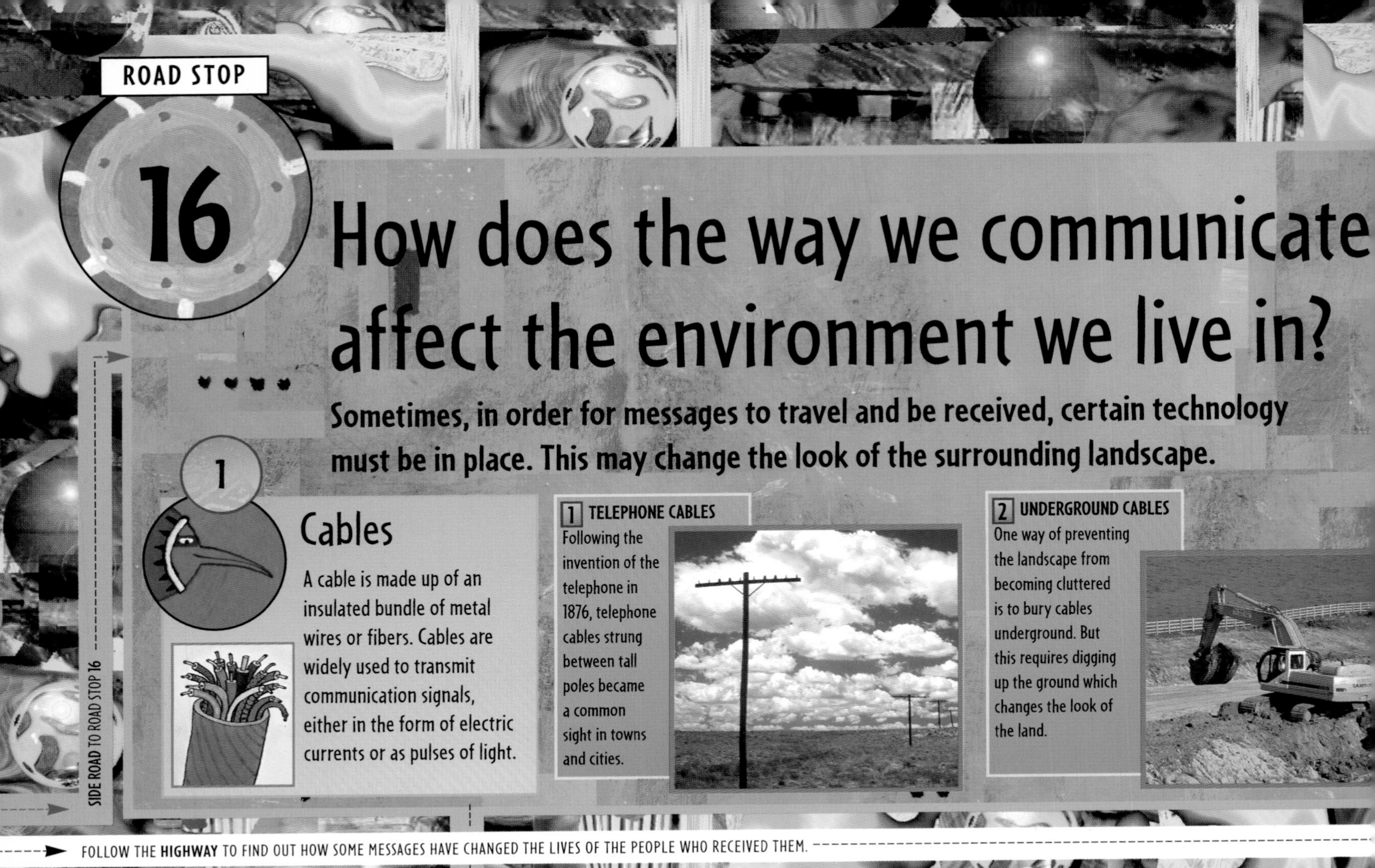

ROAD STOP

16

How does the way we communicate affect the environment we live in?

Sometimes, in order for messages to travel and be received, certain technology must be in place. This may change the look of the surrounding landscape.

1

Cables

A cable is made up of an insulated bundle of metal wires or fibers. Cables are widely used to transmit communication signals, either in the form of electric currents or as pulses of light.

1 TELEPHONE CABLES

Following the invention of the telephone in 1876, telephone cables strung between tall poles became a common sight in towns and cities.

2 UNDERGROUND CABLES

One way of preventing the landscape from becoming cluttered is to bury cables underground. But this requires digging up the ground which changes the look of the land.

SIDE ROAD TO ROAD STOP 16

FOLLOW THE **HIGHWAY** TO FIND OUT HOW SOME MESSAGES HAVE CHANGED THE LIVES OF THE PEOPLE WHO RECEIVED THEM.

SIDE ROAD TO ROAD STOP 17

3

Satellite dishes and antennas

A house or business may have an individual antenna or satellite dish, attached to its wall or roof for receiving television signals.

The world's tallest self-supporting structure is the CN Tower—a broadcasting tower in Toronto, Ontario, Canada, that rises to 1,815 feet (553 m).

Broadcasting antennas are built on tall towers, and are usually on high ground to help distribute the signals widely.

4

Advertising messages

Advertisers, eager to attract the attention of potential customers, may resort to brash gimmicks. Huge billboards, neon signs, flashing lights, video screens, and eye-catching designs may overwhelm the surrounding environment.

ROAD STOP

17

IN BRITAIN

1800's
80 percent of the population lived in the country.

1990's
90 percent of the population lives in cities.

Deto

TODAY, COMMUNIC
TECHNOLOGY ALLO
TO LIVE AND WORK
SAME PLACE. LEA
ROAD STOP 1

COMMUNICATION TECHNOLOGY HAS CHANGED THE WAY WE LIVE. **SIDE ROAD** TO ROAD STOP 17

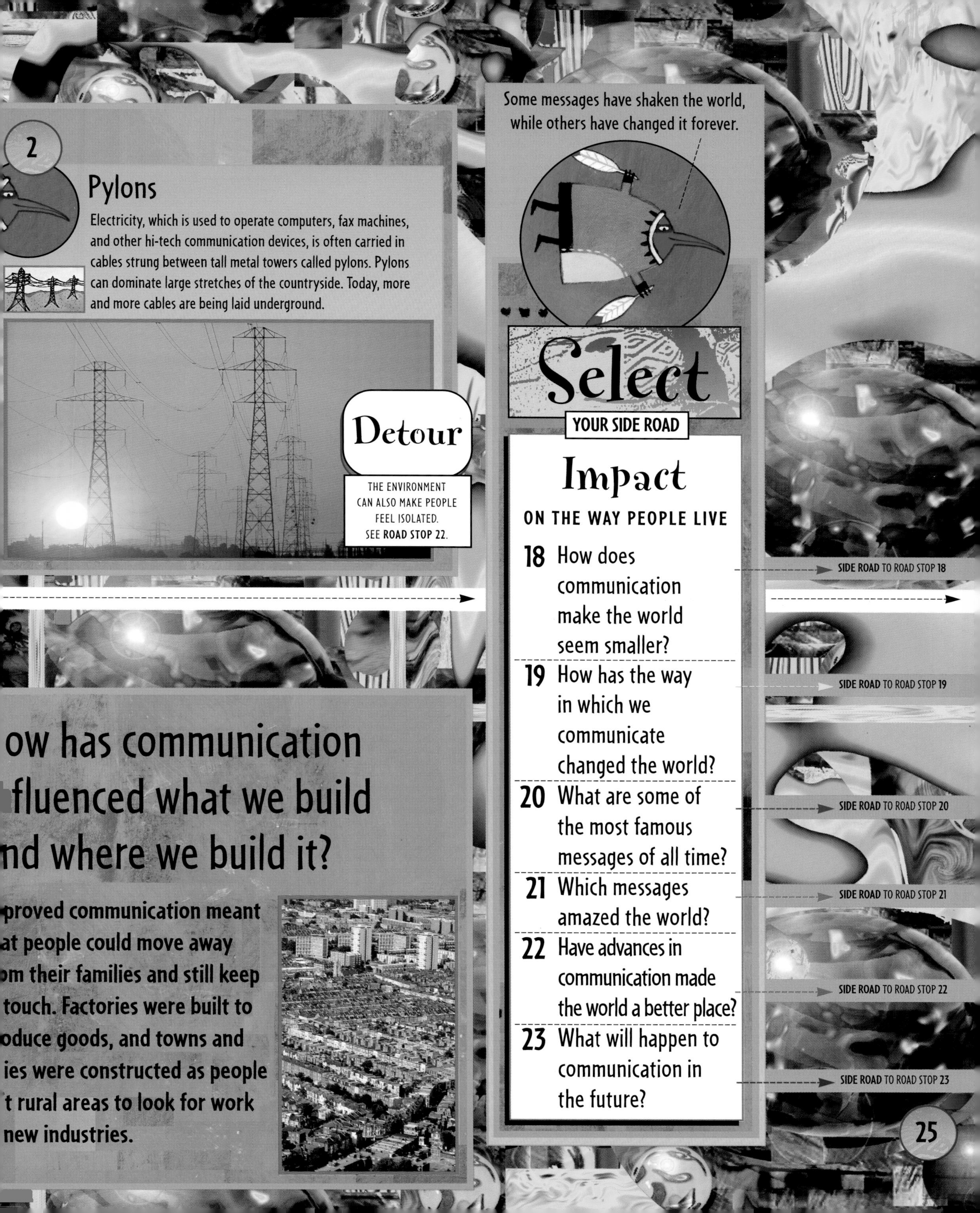

2 Pylons

Electricity, which is used to operate computers, fax machines, and other hi-tech communication devices, is often carried in cables strung between tall metal towers called pylons. Pylons can dominate large stretches of the countryside. Today, more and more cables are being laid underground.

Detour

THE ENVIRONMENT CAN ALSO MAKE PEOPLE FEEL ISOLATED. SEE **ROAD STOP 22**.

ow has communication fluenced what we build nd where we build it?

proved communication meant at people could move away om their families and still keep touch. Factories were built to oduce goods, and towns and ies were constructed as people t rural areas to look for work new industries.

Some messages have shaken the world, while others have changed it forever.

Select

YOUR SIDE ROAD

Impact

ON THE WAY PEOPLE LIVE

ROAD STOP

18

How does communication make the world seem smaller?

SIDE ROAD TO ROAD STOP 18

Telecommunication systems have helped to bridge the gap between continents. Telephones, televisions, satellites, and computers allow us to communicate almost instantly with people around the world. They give us more knowledge about how others live and what they believe in, and they make the world seem like a much smaller place.

TV TALES

THE EVENT:
The 1996 Summer Olympic Games held at Atlanta, Georgia.

DISCOVER WHETHER OR NOT COMMUNICATION IS A GOOD THING! FOLLOW THE **HIGHWAY**.

ROAD STOP

19

How has the way in which we communicate changed the world?

SIDE ROAD TO ROAD STOP 19
SIDE ROAD TO ROAD STOP 20
SIDE ROAD TO ROAD STOP 21
SIDE ROAD TO ROAD STOP 22
SIDE ROAD TO ROAD STOP 23

The advances in communication technology have influenced every aspect of our lives.

1

The way we live

TELEVISION gives us news about the world.
EFFECTS We may read less. We may travel less, learning about countries by watching TV programs rather than by visiting the places.

TELEPHONES help us to keep in touch.
EFFECTS We may write fewer letters and travel less often to see people. We may lose some of our privacy.

SOME MESSAGES HAVE BEEN REMEMBERED THROUGHOUT HISTORY. **SIDE ROAD** TO ROAD STOP 20
SOME MESSAGES CHANGED THE WORLD FOREVER. **SIDE ROAD** TO ROAD STOP 21
IS IT TIME TO STOP ADVANCING COMMUNICATION TECHNOLOGY? **SIDE ROAD** TO ROAD STOP 22
WHAT CAN WE EXPECT TO HAPPEN NEXT? **SIDE ROAD** TO ROAD STOP 23

Detour

[H]AVING LEARNED TO SEND MESSAGES AROUND THE GLOBE, WE ARE NOW [BE]AMING OUT MESSAGES TO [O]THER GALAXIES! LEAP TO **ROAD STOP 23**.

[Y]OUR EXPERIENCE:
The Games were broadcast to more than 170 countries and watched on TV by about two billion people each day.

NOT THE WHOLE PICTURE

Of course, we can only experience what is presented to us. In many cases, messages are cut, or edited, to fit into a time slot or organized to convey a particular program maker's viewpoint.

DIRECT CONTACT

☀ Being able to discuss subjects on screen with people you have never physically met also makes our planet seem like a smaller place.
☀ The Internet has paved the way for a new kind of language. Users have developed a range of symbols, known as emoticons, that can be read and understood by most people from anywhere in the world.

Visible Proof SPOT

Match the emoticons to their correct meanings.

1 User is laughing	**A** :-|
2 User is being serious	**B** |-0
3 User is yawning	**C** :-D

ANSWERS: 1=C; 2=A; 3=B.

Not everyone has access to the same technology. In developing countries, telecommunications may only be available to the rich minority. For the poorer majority, the world can still seem a big and bewildering place.

FOLLOW THE **HIGHWAY**.

2

The way we work

Detour

WHAT EFFECT COULD THIS KIND OF LIFESTYLE HAVE ON THE HUMAN RACE? LEAP TO **ROAD STOP 22**.

☀ **COMPUTERS** allow workers in different buildings, cities, and even countries to be linked.
☀ **EFFECTS** People work from home instead of from an office, communicating with each other via phones, fax machines, and computer networks.

Sometimes tradition is more important than technological advances. An example of a communication method that has remained unchanged for centuries can be found in the religion called Islam. A muezzin calls followers to prayer five times a day. His distinctive, musical chant carries far and wide from his position high up in the tower, or minaret, attached to the mosque.

SIDE ROAD TO ROAD STOP **20**
SIDE ROAD TO ROAD STOP **21**
SIDE ROAD TO ROAD STOP **22**
SIDE ROAD TO ROAD STOP **23**

20 What are some of the most famous messages of all time?

We have remembered and preserved many messages throughout history because they conveyed such important information. Sometimes, the fact that a message has been sent and received is more important than its content. Other messages are remembered for their impact on the world.

MARATHON MAN (490 B.C.)

A messenger called Pheidippides ran the 25 miles (40 km) distance from Marathon to Athens, Greece, to bring news of a Greek victory over the invading Persians. After delivering the message, he dropped dead to the floor. His feat is commemorated by the marathon, a running race of about 26 miles (42.2 km).

MAYAN MESSAGES (1100-1500)

The Mayans of Central America made fragile books from figtree bark. They used elaborate pictures called hieroglyphics to record important dates, historical events, and information about their gods. Only four of these books survived the Spanish invasion in the early 1500's. Experts are still trying to decode the mysterious symbols used in the Mayan texts.

FOLLOW THE **HIGHWAY** TO THE END OF YOUR JOURNEY.

ROAD STOP

21 Which messages amazed the world?

Messages can amaze if they upset or surprise the people receiving them. Messages may also question or overturn commonly held beliefs.

1 Religious messages

Many religions have collections of sacred writings:

CHRISTIANITY	BIBLE (left)
ISLAM	QURAN (above
JUDAISM	TORAH
BUDDHISM	TRIPITAKA
HINDUISM	VEDAS
TAOISM	TAO TE CHING

SIDE ROAD TO ROAD STOP 20

SIDE ROAD TO ROAD STOP 21

HAS ALL THIS CHANGE MADE THE WORLD A BETTER PLACE? **SIDE ROAD** TO ROAD STOP 22

IMAGINING THE FUTURE. **SIDE ROAD** TO ROAD STOP 23

BURNING BEACONS (1588)

…sh people lit …cons on hills …arnings that Spanish …ada (a fleet …rmed ships) approaching …coast, ready …nvasion. It took less than an …r for the message to travel …ss the length of the country.

TITANIC TRAGEDY (1912)

The British passenger ship the *Titanic* was supposed to be unsinkable. But on the liner's first voyage, from Southampton, England, to New York City, it struck an iceberg and sank. Over 1,500 lives were lost. Newspapers around the world reacted to the disaster with a flurry of headlines, photographs, extended reports, and special sections.

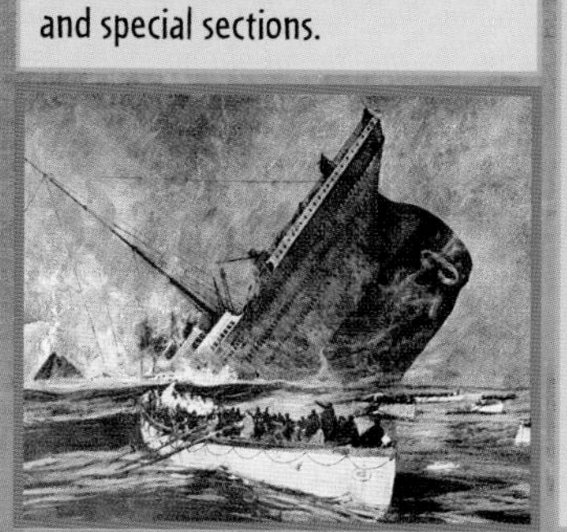

A MESSAGE FROM MARS (1938)

"Ladies and gentlemen, I have a grave announcement to make. Incredible as it may seem, strange beings who landed in New Jersey tonight are the vanguard of an invading army from Mars." Thousands of Americans panicked when they heard this radio message. But it was actually a play based on the H. G. Wells novel *The War of the Worlds*.

A SPEECH FROM SPACE (1969)

The American astronaut Neil Armstrong became the first person to set foot on the moon. He spoke to the world via satellite communication. This was his famous message: "That's one small step for a man, one giant leap for mankind."

FAMOUS FIRSTS

AUGUST 16, 1858
"Glory to God in the highest, on Earth peace, goodwill toward men."
The first official communication sent over a transatlantic cable.

MARCH 10, 1876
"Mr Watson, come here. I want you!"
The first telephone message –Alexander Graham Bell was calling for his assistant after accidentally spilling a jar of acid.

1927
"Wait a minute, wait a minute. You ain't heard nothin' yet."
Al Jolson, in the first talking film, *The Jazz Singer*.

FOLLOW THE **HIGHWAY**.

…ESSAGE: "I AM THE SON OF GOD"

…Jesus Christ lived almost 2,000 years …go in Palestine, in the Middle East. …he Christian religion is based on his life …nd teachings.

At the age of 30, Jesus began traveling …o preach his ideas about God and how …eople should live. He drew huge crowds …herever he went.

…Palestine's Roman rulers thought …sus's ideas would cause people to …bel. Jesus was arrested and executed.

During his lifetime, Jesus's message …as spread by word of mouth. After his …eath, his close followers, or disciples, …rote down his teachings in the Bible.

2 Scientific messages

Visible Proof SPOT

Whisper a message into a friend's ear. They then whisper it to the next person, who whispers it to the next, and so on. The last person to receive the message reveals it to everyone. Is this message the same as the original one sent?

MESSAGE: "ALL LIVING THINGS SHARE A FEW COMMON ANCESTORS."

- The British naturalist Charles Darwin (1809-1882) is famous for his theory of evolution. This theory states that over millions of years, all plants and animals gradually developed from a few common ancestors.
- In 1859, Darwin published his ideas in a book called *The Origin of Species*. His ideas shocked many people and caused fierce arguments.
- Even today, not everyone agrees with Darwin's theory. Some people believe that God created all living things within a short period of time.

MESSAGES ARE NOT ALWAYS UNDERSTOOD THE WAY THEY WERE INTENDED.

- In 1945, during World War II, Japan replied to a message from the United States and its allies which asked it to surrender. The Japanese wanted more time, but their badly-worded answer wrongly suggested they would ignore the warning. Some people think this failed message partly led to the bombing of the Japanese cities of Hiroshima and Nagasaki.

SIDE ROAD TO ROAD STOP 22
SIDE ROAD TO ROAD STOP 23

ROAD STOP

22

Have advances in communicatio made the world a better place?

Today, we are able to send messages quickly and in many different ways. We can easily share our knowledge and experience with others. But we need t be aware of the possible consequences of our technological advances.

PRESERVING OUR DIFFERENCES

There is a risk of losing traditional means of communication if we all send messages in the same way.

THE YALI TRIBE

THEN Irian Jaya is the western half of the Pacific island of New Guinea. Parts of it are so remote that, until fairly recently, Europeans did not know anyone lived there. The Yali tribe live in the highlands of Irian Jaya, surrounded by dense tropical forests. The jungle has long shielded them from the outside world.

NOW The Yali language and culture is being threatened as airports, satellite dishes, and telephones start to appear along the coast.

THE NORTH AMERICAN INDIANS

As recently as 200 years ago, the North American Indians spoke more than 300 different languages. Today, only 40 or so are heard much. Most of the languages failed to survive because the few people who spoke them passed away, and because of the influence of American culture and the spread of English throughout the world.

FOLLOW THE **HIGHWAY**.

ROAD STOP

23

What will happen to communication in the future?

From smoke signals and drum beats to cellular phones and the Internet, humans have always come up with more effective ways to get their messages across.

SCIENCE FICTION DREAMS?

In the future, we may evolve to such an extent that we can read each other's thoughts. We may be able to transport ourselves between places simply by imagining it. These may appear far-fetched ideas, but so did walking on the moon 100 years ago!

TINY TELEPHONES

Scientists are currently developing tiny telephones that resemble the communicators used by the crew in the 1960's television series *Star Trek*. The phones would be capable of sending and receiving both sound and pictures and may be worn as badges, bracelets, or earrings.

HOLOGRAPHIC TELEVISIONS

Technologies are emerging that will allow very thin TV screens to be built. Future televisions will be hung on walls like paintings, or even cover entire walls. Engineers are also working on holographic televisions, which use lasers to create three-dimensional images on-screen.

SIDE ROAD TO ROAD STOP 22
SIDE ROAD TO ROAD STOP 23

Visible Proof SPOT

lany of the Indian groups developed a
ommon sign language so that they
ould communicate with each other.
ıvent a sign language
f your own and use it
ɔ send messages to
our friends!

IS THERE ANYBODY OUT THERE?

laving learned how to send messages
etween continents, we have now
urned our attention to space. As part
f Project Phoenix, a worldwide search
ɔr alien life, huge radio telescopes are
argeting 200 stars for signals that
ould have been made by intelligent
fe. Plaques on the sides of the Pioneer
) and 11 space probes carry images of
eople and of the Earth's position in
ıe solar system (below).

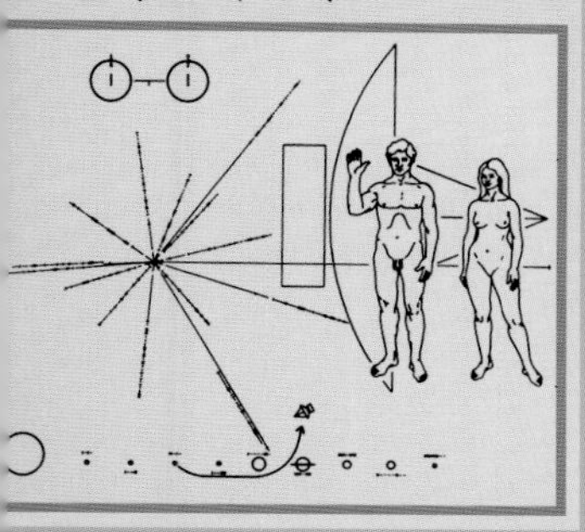

From the Brain–through space to the Impact Zone–you!

A journey that brings new ideas and discoveries, opinions, and beliefs.

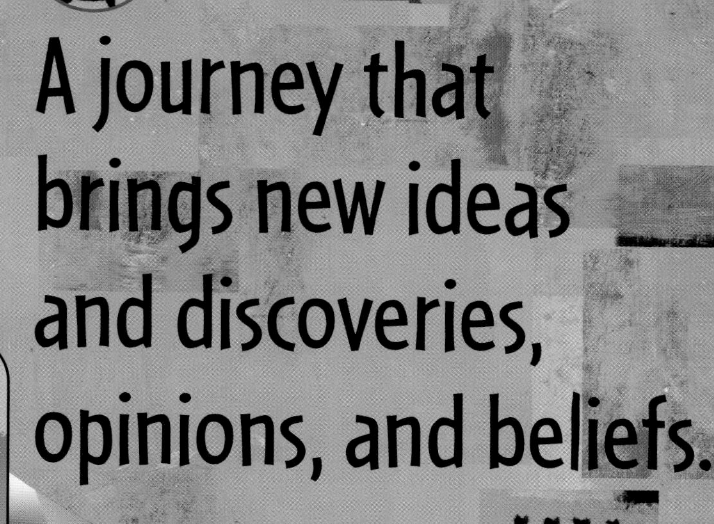

Think!

From the first grunts to the Internet and intergalactic messages–what will the next 1,000 years bring?

PICTURE CREDITS Front cover: left: Science Photo Library; center: Telegraph Colour Library; right: Ace. Back cover: Zefa. P1 background: Astrid & Hans Frieder/Science Photo Library. P3 top: David Ducros/Jerrican/Science Photo Library; bottom: Pictor. P6 background: Tony Craddock/Science Photo Library; top, bottom: Scott Camazine/Science Photo Library. P7 background: Tony Craddock/Science Photo Library; bottom: Manfred Kage/Science Photo Library; top: Zefa. P8 left: CNRI/Science Photo Library; right: Rex Features. P9 top: Custom Medical Stock Photo/Science Photo Library; bottom: Retna. P10 Bruce Iverson/Science Photo Library. P11 Tony Stone. P12 top: Tony Stone; bottom: Ancient Art & Architecture (AA&A). P13 top: US Library of Congress/Science Photo Library; center: Bridgeman Art Library; bottom: Rex Features. P14 top left: Sinclair Stammers/Science Photo Library; top right: AA&A; bottom left: Tony Stone. P15 top right: Brian Brake/Science Photo Library; bottom left: Tony Stone; bottom right: Science Photo Library. P16 top left: Mary Evans; top right: Library of Congress/Science Photo Library; bottom left: Pictor; bottom right: Advertising Archive. P17 top left, bottom right: Tony Stone; center left, center right: Science Photo Library; bottom center: Harlequins Carnival/Joan Miró 1924-25 © ADAGP, Paris & DACS, London 1997/ Bridgeman Art Library. P18 background: Tony Craddock/Science Photo Library; top: Tony Stone; center: AKG Photo; bottom left, bottom right: Mary Evans. P19 background: Tony Craddock/Science Photo Library; center: Science & Society; bottom left: Zefa; bottom right: Rosenfeld Image Ltd/Science Photo Library. P21 top left: Science & Society; top center bottom right: Mary Evans; top right: Science Photo Library; bottom left: Images; bottom center: Tony Stone. P22 left: AA&A; right: Tony Stone. P24 top left, bottom right: Tony Stone; top right: Images; bottom center: Pictor; bottom left: Zefa. P25 top: David Nunuk/Science Photo Library; bottom: Tony Stone. P26 background: Pictor; top: Allsport. P27 background, top center: Pictor; top Left, bottom left: Tony Stone; top right: Magnum Photos; bottom right: Camera Press. P28 top, bottom: AA&A. P29 top left, top center: Hulton Getty; top right: Science & Society; bottom left: AA&A; bottom center: National Library of Medicine/Science Photo Library; bottom right: Popperfoto. P30 Tony Stone. P31 NASA/Science Photo Library.